THE GOOD LIFE

THE GOOD LIFE

BY RICHARD WEBBER

ORION

Dedicated to Nan, with all my love

First published in 2000 by Orion Books
Orion House, 5 Upper St Martin's Lane
London WC2H 9EA

Pictures supplied by Don Smith,
BBC and Radio Times.

A CIP catalogue record for this book
is available from the British Library.

Printed in Trento, Italy.

CONTENTS

ACKNOWLEDGEMENTS

When you write a book like this, there are always plenty of people who help in its production. First and foremost, I would like to thank John Esmonde and Bob Larbey, the writers of *The Good Life*, who granted their permission for the book and gave up their time to be interviewed about their creation – without their co-operation, you wouldn't be reading this book now.

I also want to thank all the actors and production team members who talked about their time on the show, especially Richard Briers, Reginald Marsh, Brian Jones, producer John Howard Davies, Jimmy Gilbert, Sally Nieper, Celia McDowell, Marianne Ford, Ken Willicombe, Rita Reekie, Angela Thorne, Moyra Fraser, Tony Oxley, Oliver Elmes, Janet Pimlott and Burt Rhodes, who kindly gave permission for me to reproduce his musical score. I'm also grateful to Tricia Eddington for talking about her late husband, who played such a big part in the show's success.

Thanks are also due to many other people I spoke to, or who helped in other ways, including George Layton, Gareth Gwenlan, Jan Etherington, Edward Taylor, Peter Spence, Stanley Price, Lyn Thomas, Heather Thomas and Mark Lomas, Jane Seymour, John Seymour, John and Dorothy Barnes, Liz Wright (editor of *Smallholder* magazine), Cody Morgan, Don Smith, and to David Hamilton for checking, once again, transmission dates and cast lists. Also, the residents, past and present, of Kewferry Road, who kindly told me about what it's like loaning your house to a television company – so thanks go to Albert Carr, Barbara Appleton, John and Betty Tindall, and Margaret and Michael Mullins.

Sir Alan Ayckbourn, Peter Bowles and Sydney Lotterby contributed to this book, and I appreciate their help; many thanks, again, to Hilary Johnson, Simon Hall at the BBC, Neil Somerville at BBC Written Archives, and my agent, Jeffrey Simmons, as well as Trevor Dolby and Pandora White at Orion. And all my love to Paula, for her continued support.

RICHARD WEBBER
Clevedon, 1999

INTRODUCTION

When John and I first explained the idea for *The Good Life* to Jimmy Gilbert, who was then Head of Comedy at the BBC, he listened politely, considered for a moment and then said, 'It's very ingenious.' This could have been the cue to head for the door, but fortunately Jimmy must have seen a little more to the idea than that, as he wondered if Richard Briers might like it. To our delight, Richard did like it. John Howard Davies was appointed as producer and we were away with casting and writing the first series.

Casting is always crucial and the fates smiled on us with this one. Richard was, of course, an already popular and established television comedy lead, but we struck gold with those other three parts. Felicity Kendal, Paul Eddington and Penelope Keith were already very successful actors but – and here's the key point – none of them was known for television comedy. A huge plus, this, as they came as fresh faces to situation comedy. What we had was a dream cast of effectively four leading actors, as shown by the fact that they all went on to star in sitcoms of their own.

Strange to remember it now, but self-sufficiency was not on the original agenda for John and me. We started with the premise of a man (Tom Good) reaching forty and realizing that he was fossilizing in a job he hated, but having a dream of actually doing something with the rest of his life. But what dream? It was only then that the idea of self-sufficiency came and it all fell into place. It would be about a man and his incredibly supportive wife battling to beat the odds in a quest to create their own little self-sufficient kingdom.

Whether it was luck or ingenuity I don't know, but two key factors helped the idea succeed. First of all we decided to keep self-sufficiency rooted in the suburbs – a back garden in Surbiton is funnier than a field in Wales. Secondly, the neighbours. The Goods obviously needed some opposition, but it would have been too easy to have nasty neighbours ranting over the fence. So Jerry and Margo were born – almost totally opposed to everything Tom and Barbara tried, but old and mostly loyal friends.

Under John Howard Davies and his team, the production really was a thing of wonder. We were encouraged to write whatever we wanted and leave it to them to provide it. And my word, they did. That garden in North London (we never actually got to Surbiton) changed seasons, changed vegetables and was filled with pigs, chickens and a goat – and all courtesy of that terrific team.

The critical reception of the first series was cold to lukewarm, but happily the BBC kept faith and commissioned a second series and suddenly the viewing figures soared. Strangely enough, several television critics also seemed to change their minds about it then, so we now had a success on our hands. We wrote four series, a Christmas Special and then the crowning glory, a 'Royal Special', when the Queen came to the BBC studios to watch the show being recorded.

I think it was Penny Keith who said afterwards, 'There's nowhere to go after this,' which just about summed up the general feeling. Stories about self-sufficiency were getting harder to think up, and whilst, by now, we could quite easily have gone on just writing about the two sets of neighbours, none of us wanted the programme to dribble away from its original core. So *The Good Life* came to an end and we got out the way we wanted to – before we'd out-stayed our welcome.

By some means we had created a show which seemed to find a special place in the public affection and I'll always be grateful for that. What was *The Good Life* like to make? Fun!

BOB LARBEY *Surrey, October 1999*

John Esmonde (*left*) and Bob Larbey (*right*) return to their roots.

The first episode of *The Good Life* opened with Tom Good sitting at his breakfast table, ruing the fact that he was forty years of age. In 1975 both Bob Larbey and myself, the writers, and Richard Briers had all recently reached this age or were about to do so. I like to think that one of the pillars of the show was our positive affirmation that life begins at forty. *The Good Life* was to do with doing something about life before it throttles you.

I met somebody recently who told me he had once been a member of a political party of anarchists. It struck me as a rather self-contradictory statement. No, Tom Good had it much 'righter'. His party had only two members – himself and his wife. He was a natural anarchist, but hopefully in not too deadly serious a manner. That was another pillar of *The Good Life* – comic anarchy.

Something else central to the idea is the fact that the Goods' revolution happened in Surbiton, not somewhere in the depths of the country. I think it is much funnier to 'go back to nature' in the suburbs. The front and back gardens were dug up in The Avenue, far away from the fields. The gardens were also dug up right next door to Margo and Jerry Lead-better, two very conventionally upper-management people but friends of the Goods. The friendship bound them all together and the stress was lovely.

As one of the programme's conceivers and writers, I would like to think that we came up with some-thing funny – something funny about something. If not, I still have as a consolation the fact that, dotted around the country, there must be lots of nanny goats called Barbara or Margo.

JOHN ESMONDE *Spain, October 1999*

HISTORY OF THE SERIES

Comedy is largely ephemeral and it's only the very best examples that get to be handed down from generation to generation like some treasured family heirloom. The ranks of sitcoms that have failed the test of time and slipped quietly into obscurity far outweigh those of the glittering gems, the die-hards of the genre that live on even decades after originally gracing our screens. Only when new audiences meet the characters years later and still welcome them as warmly as the first time around can a programme be termed a true classic.

John Esmonde and Bob Larbey, one of Britain's most successful writing partnerships, have come up with more than their fair share of classics. Their output includes the likes of *Please, Sir!* and *Ever Decreasing Circles*, to name only two. However, *The Good Life* is probably their best-loved creation, partly because its central theme taps into something that most people can immediately relate to – the temptation to jack in the nine-to-five job and break free from the relentless stresses and strains of life as a commuter. When it comes to it, of course, few of us have the motivation, courage or perhaps sheer foolhardiness of Tom Good to decide that reaching the age of forty is a turning point that calls for just such radical action. But those not brave enough to take the plunge themselves could at least sit at home willing Tom on in pursuit of his idyll.

With the Leadbetters providing the perfect counterpoint to their main characters, the Goods, John Esmonde and Bob Larbey had found the ideal mix of ingredients for a first-class sitcom offering warm and polished humour – a much-needed tonic amidst a plethora of less memorable examples of comedy.

THE BIG IDEA

When Jimmy Gilbert was promoted to Head of Comedy at the BBC in the early 1970s, one of his first projects was securing a vehicle for Richard Briers. 'I wanted to find something good for him because, in my view, he was one of the best comedy actors we had.' After talking to writers John Esmonde and Bob Larbey, Gilbert asked them to think up an idea for Briers, someone they too had always admired.

One day, while John and Bob were idling away a few moments discussing the onset of middle age, the

idea they'd been looking for hit them. Since Bob had recently reached his fortieth birthday, and John wasn't far behind, they began considering whether, for some people, this age marked a crossroads in life. 'We both centred on whether it was a milestone age, when you're no longer young and have to admit that middle age has started to set in,' explains Bob. 'It didn't worry me whether I was forty or eighty, because I was happy and doing what I wanted. But it's a stage at which a lot of people start asking what they've done with their life.'

This conversation sparked off a train of thought that promised to lead to just the vehicle Jimmy Gilbert was looking for. 'We dreamt up a man who'd reached the age of forty, was doing a job he hated and felt unfulfilled. The big question he faced was what to do about it,' says Bob. The more they considered this scenario, the more they thought it was a good starting point for a sitcom. 'There's got to be some basic truth in sitcom, and we felt the idea had that. A forty-year-old realizing he was never going to be a raging success at business was an easy character to identify with.'

Sufficiently enthused by their brainchild, the next thing John and Bob had to decide was what the character would do with his new life once he'd taken the plunge and packed in his job. 'We mulled over lots of things, including him building a yacht and sailing round the world, then one of us suggested self-sufficiency,' recalls Bob. As soon as the subject was mentioned, they knew it had potential, not least because self-sufficiency was very much in vogue.

More and more people were switching on to the idea of becoming self-reliant, and a variety of articles and reports on the subject were appearing in the media. 'Plenty of people were thinking, "What can I *do* with my life instead of just going to the office every day?" But one thing was sure, they were looking for a kind of freedom,' says John.

The beauty of Esmonde and Larbey's idea was that it hadn't before been broached in situation comedy. Although the premise for the series was in itself original, their master stroke was placing the action not in some isolated spot in the countryside, but in a suburban back garden. 'If the setting had been a smallholding in Wales, it would still have been a nice idea, but not as good,' remarks Bob.

John Esmonde agrees, pointing out that it was the urban setting that created the tension – a fundamental component in any successful sitcom. 'Placing them in The Avenue, where a number of Margos and Jerrys lived up and down the road, not just next door, provided the abrasiveness. Amongst all these smart houses lived the Goods, with their front garden packed with leeks and their back yard full of pigs.'

'It was important for the location to be in the most unlikely of places,' adds Bob. 'Walk past a farmhouse in Wales and there's nothing remarkable about a garden full of vegetables, but walk past the Goods' house and you think, "What on earth is going on there?"' Even though location shooting for the series took place in Northwood, the series was firmly set in Surbiton, as Bob explains. 'To us the name epitomized London's suburbia, conjuring up the sort of neighbourhood where certain people would want to appear rather "posher" than they really were.'

The next vital ingredient in Esmonde and Larbey's successful recipe came in the form of Margo and Jerry Leadbetter. Less experienced writers might have opted for neighbours who were against everything the Goods stood for and focused the action on altercations over the garden fence – but that would have been too predictable. Instead, Bob and John chose characters who were old friends, producing even more tension by plunging the Leadbetters (albeit mainly Margo) into an emotional tug-of-war. They had been friends with the Goods for years, but their loyalty was tested to the limit when Tom and Barbara set out on their self-sufficiency drive.

For Margo, maintaining her perceived high standing in the community and keeping up with her toffee-nosed chums wasn't going to be easy living next door to nonconformists like Tom and Barbara. While she would much rather have lived beside a couple who followed a more 'normal' lifestyle (preferably Tories), she still respected the Goods and showed moments of true support and friendship. This is exemplified in the episode 'Backs to the Wall', in which Margo dons wellies to help her friends save their harvest.

'It made for a more interesting show, having the neighbours as friends. Tom had been a pal of Jerry's at the office, and you don't stop being mates because one of you seems to have gone slightly mad!' remarks John Esmonde, who feels they would have lost an awful lot if Margo had been presented as simply a virago, ranting and raving over the fence.

'As soon as we'd decided that the Goods' neighbours would play a part in the sitcom, we talked a lot about our approach,' recalls Bob. 'You immediately think of neighbours hating what the Goods are doing, but if they retain that position throughout, the momentum's got a limited life. There are only so many times you can use lines like "Oh, what's that awful smell?", so we decided they should be friends. Sure, they had their spats, and although the Lead-betters, especially Margo, disapproved of what their neighbours were doing, they remained friends – it was much more interesting than just having them complaining over the fence.'

Since neither John Esmonde nor Bob Larbey had any experience of self-sufficiency, research was key in ensuring credibility in the scripts. Although they were writing a comedy, it was important for the situations and predicaments affecting Tom and Barbara to be plausible. 'We did a fair amount of reading up on the subject,' says John. 'For example, when we were talking about what you can do with dung, such as produce methane, that had to be researched. Or how you arrive at the yarn when you're weaving, and so forth.'

Once they both felt happy with the format of the proposed sitcom, they spoke to Jimmy Gilbert at the

BBC to see if it met with his approval. Initially, Bob wasn't convinced Jimmy liked the idea. 'When we told him the plan, he replied, "Very ingenious," and for some reason we both felt he hated it.'

But they were wrong, as Gilbert himself explains. 'They had this idea about two people living in the suburbs, with the man wanting to give up the rat race and return to his roots. At first, I was concerned and said, "Oh no, he's not going back to the country, is he?" BBC2 had done a show along those lines, and programmes about the townie moving to the country can be a bit twee. They never seem to work properly. But John and Bob explained that their idea was the exact opposite, in that the couple would be giving up the rat race but staying in town. The whole point was that they were going to be self-sufficient in an urban area, which was a completely novel idea. I said it sounded promising, asked them to put it in writing, and told them that when they'd produced a couple of pages I'd send them to Richard.'

Richard Briers liked the idea and wanted to see some scripts, so Jimmy Gilbert commissioned the

writers to produce the first one, which duly met with Briers' approval. Next, Gilbert had to secure the backing of the station's controller. 'I had a good relationship with the controllers of BBC1 and BBC2, so, if there was something I was really keen on, I'd jump in the lift and go and see them. If they had the money and the studios, they would agree.

'But I always asked for a back-up script to make sure the idea wasn't just a one-off. That would have wasted everybody's time, and I didn't want to spend money and resources on the basis of a single episode. I needed either a development script that would be the second episode, or a typical episode later in the series, whatever the writers wanted to complete, to ensure it wasn't a flash in the pan.'

Being asked for another script concentrated the writers' minds, as it forced them to take the project a stage further. 'With the first script there's so much to cram into thirty minutes: a new situation, new characters, and you have to make it funny at the same time. One has to remember that it will all be fresh to the audience, who don't yet know the characters, so they won't be relaxed to begin with. It's important to get beyond that stage, so writing another script is useful.'

Once Jimmy Gilbert was confident about the sitcom's staying power, he discussed the project with the incumbent producer of BBC1, got the go-ahead, and *The Good Life* was born.

THE CHARACTERS

Writing in the *Sunday Telegraph* back in 1975, Peter Knight felt that, in Tom and Barbara Good, Esmonde and Larbey had created 'a warm, lively and essentially likeable couple'. He was right, of course. But if *The Good Life* was to succeed, it was imperative that viewers liked the Goods and sympathized with their efforts, supporting them every step of the way in their fight

for survival and independence. With the show relying largely on just four characters, any weaknesses would be magnified, so each character had to be more than two-dimensional. Depth of characterization was essential.

Bob Larbey feels that good comedy needs a serious base, and that realism plays a part in achieving that. 'When we were defining the characters, it was obvious that Tom and Barbara had to have certain in-built characteristics. For a start, they needed courage to do what they were doing, as well as mental toughness. And Barbara had to be loyal and very much in love with Tom to go along with his kind of lunacy, because, at the end of the day, she was doing it for him, not herself. I always liked the sexy bits between them – they were always dashing off to bed, sharing baths, or giving Margo ideas. For their time, Tom and Barbara were actually quite a sexy little couple.'

Producer John Howard Davies classes Tom Good as 'a pretty horrible character, with charm'. 'I never thought of him as a very nice man,' he explains, 'getting his wife to completely change her lifestyle and give everything up just for some theory of his. To balance that rather nasty side of his character he had to have charm, and it all fell into place.'

'There's an element of arrogance in Tom Good, too,' adds John Esmonde. 'We thought he needed that, to really believe in himself. In "Mr Fix-It" a journalist asks him what advice he'd give to anyone contemplating his kind of lifestyle, and Tom replies, "You have to be married to Barbara, and just sane enough to be mad." That's how we thought of him. He could be overzealous at times, while Barbara was an absolute brick. We went through the same process for all of them, and when you end up with two couples like Tom and Barbara and Margo and Jerry, played by four actors of such stunning quality, you quickly realize you don't need many other people.'

For the Leadbetters a completely different set of characteristics had to be drawn. 'That was certainly a Margo-driven household, and Jerry's behaviour was always about keeping his wife happy,' comments John Esmonde. 'He had a faintly neurotic edge to him, because of his job and responsibilities, and although he didn't like the poverty and squalor his neighbours lived in, part of him envied what they'd achieved.

'While Jerry was obviously successful and capable, Margo was the kind of wife that suited him – socially adept, and quite willing to entertain twenty Chinese businessmen at short notice. She provided the strength he needed, even though she was pretentious and thought she was too good for Surbiton.'

Snobbery was a flaw in Margo's and, to a lesser degree, Jerry's make-up, but it wasn't a theme the writers decided to explore through the sitcom. 'We needed a reason why the neighbours would be disapproving, and what better reason than snobbery? Rather than have them say lines like "I hate all the

smell and mess", we felt "This is Surbiton, and we *don't* do that type of thing here" was much stronger.'

In the original script Jerry was to be a smoker, until Paul Eddington asked the writers to rid the man of his habit. His character was also the butt of much protest from viewers. During the episode 'The Day Peace Broke Out', Jerry visits Tom in prison and calls him a 'silly sod'. 'That line caused such reaction from the fans,' recalls Bob Larbey. 'People were shocked that this word should appear in *The Good Life*. We thought we'd used it in a totally harmless way, not at all abusive, but a lot of the audience didn't see it that way.'

Although the show was originally written as a vehicle for Richard Briers, and he and his screen wife enjoyed the lion's share of the early episodes, the neighbours were so well defined – and brilliantly

played – that they soon became stars in their own right. 'Particularly Margo,' admits Bob Larbey. 'She became hugely popular as a character. It was always intended to be a foursome, because you needed that. The Goods were perfectly funny on their own, but there's a limit to what you can do with only two characters and a load of chickens. To keep the conflict going, we needed other strong characters, but Margo just grew and grew.'

Bob likes to feel that the strength of the scripts, backing up Penelope Keith's brilliant acting, helped create this situation. 'Penelope was absolutely wonderful as Margo. Scenes she was in have been talked about for years, and she was the funniest character by a long way. But it was simply the way it turned out, the way it was written. John and I didn't set out to make her hugely funny, but we soon realized that she was the funniest character. They could all get laughs,

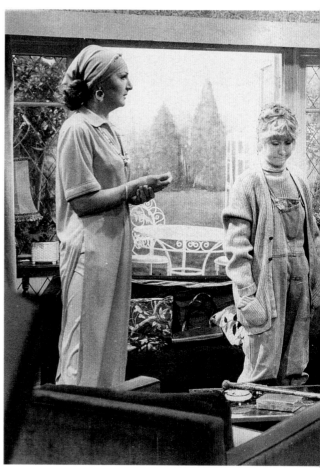

but when Margo came into the room you were ready to laugh straight away, partly because you knew she was likely to launch into some tirade about Miss Mountshaft or something. The others, meanwhile, would feel their way through the comedy moments as they were written. But if Tom, for example, came through the door, you didn't automatically expect him to say something outrageously funny.'

Producer John Howard Davies also acknowledges that the Leadbetters grew as the series progressed. 'Quite often that happens, where the leads drive the series along but other people come in for little diamonds every now and again and steal the show – although they didn't do it every week. It's important that you have that kind of balance, though, because it gives you a release from the driving of the plot.'

THE PRODUCER – AND HIS RIGHT-HAND MAN

When it came to deciding who would direct and produce *The Good Life*, Jimmy Gilbert knew the ideal person. 'John Howard Davies was an executive producer and seemed the perfect candidate. He's a very skilful comedy producer, and experienced at creating the sort of atmosphere that actors enjoy working in, which is very important. He's confident, good at building up a team and great fun – I couldn't have chosen a better person.'

When offered the job of directing and producing the show, John Howard Davies didn't hesitate in accepting. 'If I'm honest, the chance of working with Richard Briers was very appealing,' he admits. 'But I was also interested because self-sufficiency was a popular concept back then. Books had even been published on the subject because so many people were looking for an alternative lifestyle, although most of them soon realized how impractical it was. But it was a good idea, something I felt I could get my teeth into, and working with Richard Briers into the bargain, it was a very attractive package.'

Brian Jones was recruited as John Howard Davies' right-hand man on *The Good Life*, and he enjoyed working with the producer. 'He was so kind and helpful. He had a good way with him, getting everyone to contribute in some small way. He knew what he wanted, how to get the best out of people, and was very supportive towards the actors. Initially he'd say, "That was good, but wouldn't it be an idea if you thought along *these* lines…?", but it wasn't long before the actors got into their characters, and John needed to guide them less and less.'

As far as John Howard Davies is concerned, *The Good Life* is undoubtedly one of the happiest shows he's worked on. 'I don't think anyone uttered a cross word throughout the entire period we were working on the programme. It's unbelievable, I know, but there wasn't even the hint of any temperament from the stars – or the director! It was lovely.'

Team spirit is vitally important, in John's view. 'I remember, once, a cameraman or sound man raising his voice to a colleague, and before I could say anything he'd been thrown out of the studio. They weren't allowed to show disquiet or irritation, which I think is a good thing. I can't work with people who shout at me – some people like working with a little bit of aggro in the atmosphere, but I think it's pointless.'

John assembled his own production team, many of whom stayed throughout the lifespan of the sitcom. 'I always try to keep to the same team,' he explains. 'If you get a good production team, you hang on to them, because each person knows how the others work, and that saves so much time. When you're working with people you know, you don't have to keep checking on things. Jobs get done automatically.'

One of the people who remained with the team throughout was Brian Jones, who had just finished a stint on *Crackerjack* when he heard about the new project for Richard Briers. 'I was walking down a corridor at the BBC when John's assistant spotted me. We got chatting, and she mentioned the new sitcom and suggested I pop in to see John.'

Brian, who had been a trainee floor manager when he first worked with Richard Briers on *Marriage Lines*, was given a copy of Esmonde and Larbey's script and told to visit the theatre. 'John asked whether I'd seen any shows in the West End recently, and I said, "No, but I'm willing to go." He then suggested, "Go and have a look at Penny Keith and Felicity Kendal, because they're the two female leads." From there he offered me the chance to work on the show.'

CASTING

With Richard Briers already in the bag, John Howard Davies' efforts were directed towards finding actors for the three remaining roles. It's difficult now to imagine anyone else playing the characters brought to life so expertly by Penelope Keith, Paul Eddington and Felicity Kendal. However, if things had turned out differently, Peter Bowles might have been cast as Jerry Leadbetter and Hannah Gordon as Barbara.

'I asked Peter to play Jerry,' says John Howard Davies, 'but he wouldn't because he wanted to do a play at the Crucible, so I chose Paul Eddington instead – which turned out the happiest of choices. In my opinion, he was better than anybody else could have been. He was wonderful.'

'Hannah Gordon was considered for the Felicity Kendal part, but she'd just finished doing a television series and felt the character was a bit too similar to

the one she'd just played,' recalls Jimmy Gilbert. 'But when I saw Felicity Kendal and Penny Keith on stage together in *The Norman Conquests*, I knew they'd be ideal for the parts of Barbara and Margo.'

At the same time, writers John Esmonde and Bob Larbey – who were involved in all the discussions regarding casting – had seen an actress in a TV commercial whose name they didn't know, but who they thought might be right for the part of Margo Leadbetter. During a meeting they started considering names and Bob asked who the woman was in the Benson and Hedges advertisement. 'She was appearing in the West End at the time,' he explains, 'but all

we knew her from, shamefully, was the ad, in which someone lights up and she says, "Ah… Benson and Hedges." I really liked it.'

To check whether the writers were in fact thinking of Penelope Keith, the same actress who was appearing in the Ayckbourn plays, Jimmy Gilbert turned to his copy of *Spotlight*, the casting directory. 'I wanted to make sure we were talking about the same person, and fortunately we were – it was an extraordinary coincidence.'

Apart from Richard Briers, the rest of the cast were relatively new to situation comedy, which was a plus in Bob Larbey's opinion. 'That was part of the magic.

You had three thumping good actors who weren't yet familiar to television viewers. A lot of people even thought we'd discovered them, that they were new to the profession!'

It didn't take long for the team to gel, and one of the strengths of the show is the ease with which the performers worked together, the interplay between them representing ensemble playing at its best. Jimmy Gilbert was pleased with each of the actors in their own right. 'Comedy is such a tightrope. You've got to be real and likeable all the time, as well as having razor-sharp timing and technique. There aren't many people who know how to walk

that particular tightrope, but Richard Briers does it brilliantly.

'I've worked with Richard quite a bit, and I've always admired his work. The first programme we did together was *The Seven Faces of Jim*, with Jimmy Edwards, back in 1961. I think it was Frank Muir who first told me about Richard and said I should watch out for him.

'I didn't cast Paul Eddington, but I was delighted when John Howard Davies did. I first saw him in *A Severed Head* back in the 1960s, and I'd made a mental note then that some day I wanted to work with him, which I did in *The Seven Faces of Jim*. He'd done a bit of comedy, but *The Good Life* was his big break in the genre – he was a very good actor.

'Felicity and Penelope had good reputations and had done lots of theatre work,' says Jimmy, who used to rely on the theatre for the majority of his casting. 'I went to the theatre at least once a week, and I never worried about whether an actor could transfer their skills to television. It's up to the director to make sure they tone their performance down a little, but if they've got talent, they're not going to lose it on TV.'

John Howard Davies had never worked with Keith, Kendal or Eddington, but he enjoyed the experience. 'I was so pleased with their performances that when I was promoted to Head of Comedy I gave them their own series. Paul Eddington got *Yes, Minister*, Felicity Kendal *Solo* and Penelope Keith *To the Manor Born*.'

For the writers, who sweated over the scripts for months, it must be demoralizing if actors fail to add the degree of colour and vitality expected. But that was never the case on *The Good Life*. 'They were extremely good at their jobs, obviously had talent, and didn't try any tricks with the sitcom – they simply acted it. They brought a depth to the characters that I didn't even know was there,' remarks Bob Larbey. 'For example, Penny had a wonderful gift for making the unbearable Margo very touching. She could make you feel sorry for her, like the time she admitted to not having a sense of humour.'

Some people felt it was Margo who became the 'star' of the show, the most prominent character, and she may indeed have stolen the show in a number of scenes, but production manager Brian Jones feels that the series never lost sight of its original aim. 'You always had to keep the self-sufficiency angle. You could exploit the Margo Leadbetter character and her relationship with everybody, including workmen, but you couldn't lose sight of the fact that it was still called *The Good Life* and was principally about the Goods trying to live off the land. If the writers had tried doing anything else, I don't think it would have worked. The show would have deteriorated if they'd moved away from the original theme.'

THE DAY
I TURNED
DOWN JERRY

No one can now imagine anyone being better suited than Paul Eddington to play the hen-pecked Jerry Leadbetter. As soon as he was cast in the part, he made it his own, injecting a touch of sarcasm and vulnerability into the character. But Paul was not, in fact, the first choice of producer John Howard Davies. He originally wanted PETER BOWLES to play the part – as the actor explains:

At the time, I'd done a tremendous amount of tele-vision and no theatre for eleven years, and I made a decision to start working on the stage again. The very next day, as if by an act of God, I received two offers: one was the part in *The Good Life* and the other a new Alan Ayckbourn play, *Absent Friends*. I knew I had to do the theatre. It was a good part and just the sort of opportunity I'd been looking for, so I accepted it.

When I arrived at rehearsal on the first day I saw Richard Briers, who was also in the play. He came over and asked why I'd turned down *The Good Life*. I replied, 'How do you know that?' and he said,

'Because I'm doing it.' I didn't see how that was possible, so I asked, 'How can you, Richard? I turned it down because I'm doing this play.' He then told me they were recording on Sundays. I'd never done a situation comedy before and no one had explained that to me, so I'd simply told the BBC that I was doing a play and wouldn't be free. And by now, of course, it was too late to do anything about it, because Paul Eddington had already been cast.

Absent Friends ran for a year, and during that time two series of *The Good Life* were recorded. As a joke, Richard would tease me by knocking on my dressing-room door and saying, "Hello, Peter. Just to let you know I've had another big cheque for *The Good Life*." I had to act with Richard for a year while he recorded two series of the sitcom, a pro-gramme I could have easily been involved in.

In hindsight, playing Jerry would have altered my career. He was a rather put-upon character who was dominated by his wife, and I'd played that sort of role before. What I hadn't played – ever – was a romantic lead, and if I'd done *The Good Life* I'd never have been offered *To the Manor Born*, as there's no way I could have played Penelope Keith's screen husband in two separate sitcoms.

When I was offered *To the Manor Born*, at the age of forty-three, it changed my life. For the first time I was able to stop doing the bumbling, put-upon roles and play proper romantic leads. At the time it was a little frustrating to think I could have been in *The Good Life*, but I've never regretted turning down the part of Jerry Leadbetter.

PETER BOWLES

THE FIRST READ-THROUGH

When actors, writers and producers assemble for the initial read-through, there's an inevitable nervousness, especially if it's the first time many have worked together. When everyone met to discuss 'Plough Your Own Furrow', *The Good Life*'s opening instalment, Richard Briers was excited, yet slightly anxious, because he had the lion's share of lines to deliver.

'In that first episode, the neighbours were hardly there, and in fact Margo wasn't even seen – she was just a voice-over. So it was really left to Felicity and me, with Tom doing most to establish the plot, as far as the viewers were concerned. I did a lot of the spadework, in every sense of the word. Bearing the brunt of the script meant I was very nervous; it was my responsibility to get the show on the road, making sure everyone understood what it was about.

'Gradually the Leadbetters developed as characters, and the boys [Esmonde and Larbey] realized what a marvel they'd created in Margo and Jerry as two wonderful double-acts emerged. When they got fed up with the Goods, they'd cut to next door, and vice versa. It was a profitable situation, and gradually the team became a real quartet.'

For writer John Esmonde the first read-through is always an exciting time, though sometimes a little worrying, and he always attends. 'It's very important, because it's the first time you see and hear your little baby, which is how I used to think of a new show, in the mouths of actors. Read-throughs are wonderful – the excitement never fades.' If any reworking was necessary, John and Bob would always try sorting the scripts out there and then. 'We'd change, add or delete on the day, which meant the actors and director finished the day with the script they'd be putting out at the end of the week. They didn't have to wait a few days while we amended the scripts back at the office.'

Bob Larbey feels that the read-throughs went smoothly because it was an unselfish team. 'They'd all work for each other, and if ever we were struggling and looking for cuts, Richard was one of the first to look for cuts in his own dialogue. Not many top-billing actors will do that – on the contrary, they'll fight to the death to keep their lines. But everyone worked well together from day one, so it was a joy attending read-throughs.'

THE FIRST EPISODE

For both John Esmonde and Bob Larbey, watching the first episode being transmitted on 4 April 1975 was an anxious time. 'You're always in a sort of nervous state, smiling to whoever might be in the room until your cheeks hurt, and then, afterwards, talking too much, gabbling, or just being generally nervous,' admits John. 'It's never until a few weeks later that I feel in a position to review how the programme has worked.'

When he was calm enough to collect his thoughts, John was pleased with the early episodes of *The Good Life*. 'I thought they were ever so good. We had good actors and a terrific director, a very professional team. It was a nice feeling going to work, so to speak.' At that time their place of work was a flaky, dispiriting £4-a-week Dorking office, hardly an environment befitting two of the nation's best writers of comedy. But such austere surroundings were conducive to scriptwriting, as far as Esmonde and Larbey were concerned, because there were no distractions.

They followed a particular routine, starting work late morning and finishing early evening. 'We always had an excuse for not working long days,' says Bob, recalling a piece of advice they'd been given by Frank Muir. 'What he said was, "If you're having a really good day, and you're in the middle of a purple patch, don't get sucked into writing through to midnight,

CAST LIST

TOM G OOD	–	RICHARD BRIERS
BARBARA GOOD	–	FELICITY KENDAL
JERRY	–	PAUL EDDINGTON
MARGO	–	PENELOPE KEITH
SIR	–	REGINALD MARSH
BRIAN	–	MARTIN NEIL
COMMISSIONAIRE	–	NORMAN ATKYNS

EXTRAS

PHILIP COMPTON

MICHAEL BRYDON

MARK CALLAN

FRANKLIN ARBISON

CAMERA SCRIPT   BBC–1   STUDIO T.C.8.
                                     PROJECT NO: 1144/3644

"THE GOOD LIFE"
by
JOHN ESMONDE & BOB LARBEY
Episode one
Plough Your Own Furrow

PRODUCER	JOHN HOWARD DAVIES
P.A.	BRIAN JONES
ASSISTANT	ANGELA SHARP
A.F.M.	IAIN McLEAN
FLOOR ASSISTANT	CLIVE SWAN
DESIGNER	PAUL MUNTING
COSTUME SUPERVISOR	RITA REEKIE
MAKE–UP SUPERVISOR	MARIANNE FORD
T.M.1.	RON KOPLICK
T.M.2.	HARRY BRADLEY
SOUND SUPERVISOR	LAURIE TAYLOR
GRAMS OPERATOR	NEIL SUDWICK
VISION MIXER	TONY ROWE

CREW 20

S C H E D U L E

SUNDAY 16TH MARCH
1030–1300	....	Camera Rehearsal with TK
1300–1400	....	LUNCH
1400–1830	....	Camera Rehearsal with TK
1830–1930	....	DINNER
1830–2000	....	Sound and vision line–up
TELERECORD		
2000–2130	....	VTC/6HT/98329

VT EDITING	Monday, 24th March 1930–2330
TRANSMISSION	Friday, 4th April 2030–2100

	ACTION	SOUND
(ON TK)		
MIX TO	SCENE 1. INT. "THE BIG ROOM" DAY.	
MLS TABLE		

(THIS IS A BIG ROOM AND THE CENTRE OF TOM AND BARBARA GOOD'S ACTIVITIES. IT HAS A COMFORTABLE LOUNGING-ABOUT PART, A BUREAU, LOTS OF BOOKSHELVES, AN UPRIGHT PIANO, A LARGE BRICK FIREPLACE AND A BREAKFAST TABLE AND CHAIRS BY FRENCH WINDOWS WHICH OVERLOOK A SLABBED PATIO AND A LARGE GARDEN BEYOND IT.

THE FURNISHINGS ARE ANGLED TOWARDS COMFORT AS OPPOSED TO ANY PRISTINE ELEGANCE. THERE IS A MARKED ABSENCE OF "THE CHINESE GIRL" TYPE OF REPRODUCTION – INDEED, THE PAINTINGS AND KNICK-KNACKS LOOK LIKE THEY WERE CHOSEN AS THOUGHTFUL PRESENTS INSTEAD OF DECOR OBJECTS.

THERE IS AN OPEN SERVING HATCH TO THE KITCHEN.

TOM GOOD SITS AT THE BREAKFAST TABLE, DRINKING COFFEE. ALSO ON THE TABLE IS A LARGE BIRTHDAY CAKE WITH A SINGLE, LIT CANDLE. TOM IS LOOKING THROUGH A PILE OF BIRTHDAY CARDS WHICH SEEM TO BE MOSTLY OF THE COMIC VARIETY.)

MS TOM

TOM.
(READING FROM ONE) "Mozart and Mendelssohn were dead by forty. Why aren't you?" How thoughtful.

MLS TOM

(HE LOOKS AT ANOTHER FUNNY CARD THEN TOWARDS THE SERVING HATCH)

MS TOM

TOM.
You bitch!

MLS HATCH

(BARBARA LOOKS THROUGH THE HATCH)

(3 next)

–1–

because the chances are that by then the purple patch will have gone off rather badly." He told us to try leaving a script at an interesting point, so that it's easy to get back into your work next day. It was sound advice.'

Bob also enjoyed watching the first episode, back in 1975. 'I liked it. It was slow getting off the ground, because it was establishing itself. This didn't go down too well with certain members of the press and it didn't receive a huge reception. But as soon as Tom Good put the rotavator into the lawn at the end of the episode, you could tell there would be a spark of interest in the series. People asked, "Are they really going to be this outrageous in suburbia?" And, of course, they were.'

The BBC conducted an audience survey, where a viewing panel completed questionnaires about the show, providing a valuable finger on the pulse of public opinion. The response to 'Plough Your Own Furrow' was uncertainty about the sitcom's potential. As the Audience Research Department reported on 18 April 1975, there seemed to be some variation of opinion as to whether or not this first episode held the promise of a really entertaining series. While forty per cent of the viewing panel had found it amusing, and were 'looking forward to the next round', a larger proportion reserved judgement, having been 'at best only mildly amused'. Comments ranged from 'This first episode was rather disappointing, slow and only moderately funny' to 'It wasn't very scintillating, but there were a few laughs and the situation was different from other situation comedies.' However, the majority of viewers agreed that no fault could be pinned on the actors' performances. Many were glad to see Richard Briers again, and felt that he and Felicity Kendal were 'well matched'.

Even though the first episode had met with an uncertain reception, future Audience Research Reports would reflect the public's growing acceptance of

Esmonde and Larbey's sitcom. As Peter Knight wrote in the *Sunday Telegraph* in 1975, '*The Good Life* has emerged as one of the most quietly amusing and entertaining shows of the rather stunted crop of new situation comedies, and at least it has a new idea at its core.' And the theme certainly struck a chord with viewers, even from day one. The audience survey revealed that Tom Good hankered after 'the kind of life a lot of us would like to live' and the episode 'appealed so much because this is the pipe dream of so many of us'.

Today, sitcoms can't afford to be slow starters. If they fail to make an immediate impact, they're unlikely to be given a second chance. John Esmonde was grateful to the BBC for continuing to believe in *The Good Life*. 'The audience figures weren't tremendous, and it wasn't until the third series that they

British Broadcasting Corporation   Confidential

AN AUDIENCE RESEARCH REPORT

(Week 14)   VR/75/198

THE GOOD LIFE

by John Esmonde and Bob Larbey

Producer: John Howard Davies

Friday, 4th April. 1975.   8.30-9.00-m,   BBC-1

1. Size of audience (based on results of the Survey of Listening and Viewing).

It is estimated that the audience for this broadcast was 11.6% of the United Kingdom population. Programmes on BBC-2 and ITV at the time were seen by 1.3% and 24.5% (average).

2. Reaction of audience (based on 130 questionnaires completed by 9% of the Viewing Panel).

The reactions of this sample of the audience were distributed as follows:-

A+ %	A %	B %	C %	C- %
5	31	46	15	3

giving a Reaction Index of 55.

3. There seemed some variation of opinion among the sample as to whether or not this first episode held out hopes of a really entertaining series. About two in five apparently found it very amusing, and were much looking forward to 'the next round'. It seemed to them 'completely different from the usual comedy'; the theme struck an answering chord; Tom Good hankered after 'the kind of life a lot of us would like to live' and the episode 'appealed so much because this is the pipe dream of so many of us'. It was very well handled, they said, in a witty script with 'some very funny lines'; it seemed 'made for Richard Briers'; 'a promising beginning; this could be a really funny series'.

4. A rather larger proportion of those reporting appeared to be reserving judgement, having been at best only mildly amused. Their verdicts tended to be on the following lines:-

'Promising material for a new series: real characters and a believable situation; this first episode, however, was rather disappointing, slow and only moderately funny'.

'It wasn't very scintillating, but there were a few laughs and the situation was different from other situation comedies'.

'It was quietly funny, with the promise that it is obviously going to get funnier. It was paving the way, so to speak'.

'Not quite sure but think the series could grow on one'.

'The plot shows some promise, although the first episode was rather boring'.

5. A minority, however, were less hopeful, judging from this episode which seemed to them rather silly, 'childish', tedious and unfunny. As one of them commented:

'The script was weak, the laughs few and far between; another mediocre comedy series, with the same boring theme'.

Continued/........

became huge. But those were the days when, instead of taking the show off, the BBC would say, "No, keep going, you've got something here." They gave you the opportunity to fail, the right to fail but learn from it, which was so valuable to writers.'

WORKING WITH THE ANIMALS

When it came to location filming, a collection of animals had to be herded in each day. 'All the animals were delightful, especially the little piglets,' recalls Richard Briers. 'They were so enchanting and sweet. I got so fond of them I couldn't eat bacon for about six months after recording the programme!

'There was one episode where Tom was seen in a pen with a boar. I suddenly realized that he had these frightening tusks, and when he started giving me some strange sideways looks, I got out of the pen as quickly as possible. It was only a pig, but it weighed a ton.'

Production manager Brian Jones also remembers the time Richard Briers (known to everyone as Dickie) had to venture inside the pen with the 35-stone boar. 'This pig was massive, and Dickie hadn't seen it when John Howard Davies explained the scene, which involved him entering the pen to feed the pigs. Dickie said, "Yes, right-oh. Where's the pig?", and John replied, "It's in the pen." Dickie looked but couldn't see the animal because the side of the pen was blocking his view. Then John said, "Right, we'll have a rehearsal. Off you go Dickie – and cue!"

ACTING LIKE AN ANIMAL...

Guest appearances in Tom and Barbara's menagerie were made by:

Pinky & Perky, the pigs
Lenin, a cockerel
Margo, the first goat Tom and Barbara own
Geraldine, a goat described as a 'little rhinoceros in goat's clothing'
Olivia, a chicken that Tom and Barbara serve up for their evening meal in 'Suit Yourself'
Glenda, a hen mentioned in 'When I'm 65' (who sounds like Max Wall when she clucks)
Brian, an old white horse presented to the Goods by Mr Betts, the coalman

NAMES & PLACES

You'd think it would be easy deciding on a handful of characters' names, where they live, and so on, but many writers spend days, weeks, even months deliberating over such decisions. And Esmonde and Larbey are no exception.

'One of the funny things about thinking up names for fictional characters is that, as soon as you suggest one, it sounds totally unlikely,' says Bob, who admits that they dreamt up the names Tom and Barbara Good before finding a title for the series. 'We called the characters Tom and Barbara and thought of the surname afterwards. Then the title became one of those screamingly obvious things, and we wondered why we hadn't thought of it in the first place. But titles are like that.'

John and Bob have no idea where the name Leadbetter came from. 'I haven't a clue,' says John with a shrug, 'but it has a certain poshness about it.'

'I don't know where that one came from, either,' adds Bob. 'But the name Margo instantly sounded right for the character and was a good name to say. Jerry, though, was a joke initially. We thought, we've got Tom, so we might as well have Jerry to go with him. But, again, the name seemed to suit.'

Once all the characters' names had been finalized, they had to decide on a name for where they lived. 'The Avenue sounded right for a place where self-sufficiency *shouldn't* be going on,' recalls Bob, 'rather like The Close in *Ever Decreasing Circles*. It sounded like a little empire, a little enclave, and was just right for what went on in the show.

'You can get totally bogged down on names, if you're not careful,' Bob points out. 'You think of one that sounds wrong, the next one seems equally unlikely, and it just goes on and on. In my experience, as soon as you write it down on paper it becomes a totally acceptable name – and you realize you've wasted all that time debating it!'

'Dickie said his lines, opened the pen and walked in, but as soon as he saw the pig he shouted "Jesus Christ!" before turning round and hurrying straight out again. "What is *that*?", he asked John. John's reply was simply, "Yes, it is a bit big, isn't it? But that's the size of pigs around here." But it turned out that the pig loved apples, so we were able to feed him up and eventually the scene was successfully shot.'

One of the most memorable scenes involving an animal appeared in the 1977 episode 'Our Speaker Today', which saw Tom Good in hot pursuit of Lenin, the escaped cockerel, who jumps on a bus heading for Kingston. When the cockerel was brought on the scene, Richard thought 'Christ, it's Walt Disney time!' What he didn't know was that John Howard Davies had put some hens on the bus, as well as sprinkling chicken feed inside. The cockerel didn't hesitate in jumping onto the bus, which took Richard by surprise, as he explains. 'Luckily, I was dressed and had

my boots on, but as the bus moved away I nearly had a heart attack trying to catch it. I thought I was going to be there all day, so I couldn't believe how smoothly everything went. It was an amusing scene.'

THE TITLES

Graphic designer Oliver Elmes was responsible for creating the simple yet effective opening titles, showing a white bird flying round a yellow sun before it turns into a flower, with a bee buzzing across the screen. In a way, this epitomized the 'getting back to basics' foundation of the sitcom, and Oliver, who retired from the BBC in 1990 after 25 years' service, believes that the style of credits suited the programme. 'I'm fond of that piece of work. It wasn't, in any way, a breakthrough in design brilliance, but it was very suitable for the programme.'

Another factor behind the success of the credits, as far as the BBC was concerned, was the low cost of their production. 'My department was trying to cut costs at that particular time, so we were being persuaded to use our own resources, otherwise I might have gone outside and ended up with a completely different conception,' remarks Oliver. 'I used an in-house animator, Janet Pimlott, who did a great job.'

Janet, who joined the BBC in the early 1960s and took early retirement in 1983, used to work closely with the graphic design team. 'We always discussed projects the department were working on,' she says. 'If they wanted my help, I'd listen to their thoughts and ideas before going away and charting everything up. For *The Good Life* Oliver thought up the idea and produced some sketches, and I helped develop them and worked out how we'd move the images and create the animation. I had to figure out how the bird would fly around the flower, with the petals turning into the name and the bee buzzing around. I think the outcome must have suited the programme very well, since so many people remember the opening titles sequence.

'Once everyone was happy with the plans, I took them along to Zephyr Films, the company in Chiswick that owned the rostrum cameras we used. I took all the artwork over there and we shot the opening title sequences. Beforehand, I would have marked out a camera chart with all the moves and someone would film it all,' explains Janet.

The sequence was shot in two exposures: first, the bird was filmed flying around, with cells being moved as the bird's wings flapped every four frames. 'When it reached the bottom of the flower, it glided about before flapping around the top again. Then we exposed the petals dropping and the lettering "Richard Briers in *The Good Life*". This had to be charted very carefully to synchronize with the other exposure of the bird and prevent the bird flying over the lettering, or anything awful like that.'

Oliver's design was influenced by a cartoon he had seen. 'It was a UPA cartoon called something like *The Unicorn in the Garden*. The opening

titles showed a bird flying around upside down, and that sparked off the idea. I wanted to do something similar, but in a totally different style.'

Prior to the advent of the sophisticated computer technology that now aids the work of graphic designers and animators, titles were shot using rostrum cameras and the job would have to be completed within a day. Once the producer, John Howard Davies, had given his approval, the film was ready for the programme's launch.

THE SIGNATURE TUNE

Until Ronnie Hazlehurst was appointed music adviser to Light Entertainment at the BBC in the late 1960s, most signature tunes for situation comedies were written by two or three people. Ronnie persuaded the producers to accept a new system, whereby jobs were put out to tender to as many as fifty arranger/composers as soon as a new sitcom was

Ext. 2907/8

Ref: 35/LE/RH

BRITISH BROADCASTING CORPORATION
TELEVISION CENTRE WOOD LANE LONDON W12 7RJ
TELEPHONE 01-743 8000 TELEX: 265781
TELEGRAMS AND CABLES: TELECASTS LONDON TELEX

28th January 1975.

Dear Bul,

A signature tune is required by BBC Television for a situation comedy series entitled "THE GOOD LIFE".

If you would care to submit one or more pieces for consideration by the Producer, I should be more than pleased if you would bear in mind the following:-

1.   Study carefully the attached brief.

2.   Tune(s) should be in <u>playable</u> piano form <u>only</u> at this stage (no tapes please).

3.   Careful note should be made of the metronomic timing and the combination you have in mind (maximum 8 players) for eventual recording.

4.   Submission(s) to be in my office not later than noon, Wednesday <u>19th February 1975</u>.

All rejected material will be returned as soon as possible, and the rights of such material will naturally remain with the Composer. The BBC Copyright Department will, of course, enter into the usual contract with the writer of the tune selected by the Producer.

Good luck and best wishes.

Yours sincerely,

Hilary Woxall

(Ronnie Hazlehurst)
Music Adviser,
Light Entertainment Group.

hw
Encl.

<u>N.B.</u>   Any submission containing a reference (however obscure) to the recognised tune entitled "The Good Life" (composed by Sacha Distel, Published by K.P.M.Music) will automatically be rejected on Copyright grounds.

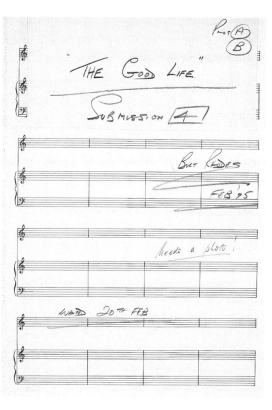

commissioned. Burt Rhodes, who went on to write the tune for *The Good Life*, was one of those fifty. 'Well-known backroom boys who had worked on orchestrations and composing were included, and everyone was allowed to submit one or more titles,' he recalls.

Along with the late Dennis Wilson, a talented pianist who also wrote many signature tunes, Burt had the task of playing all the submissions on piano and recording them. 'There were hundreds of titles

With an eight-man band, including many respected figures from the big-band world, Burt recorded the tune in a music studio at Lime Grove. From there, it was linked to Oliver Elmes' visuals. A memorable theme tune adds the finishing touch to a show, and Burt Rhodes' effort did just that for *The Good Life*. As David Thomas wrote in the *Sunday Express* back in 1993: 'The moment one heard that plinkety-plink theme tune, there was always the danger of being lost in twee suburban jollity.'

BURT RHODES

Born in the Yorkshire town of Guiseley in 1923, Burt played the organ at local churches and performed with various dance bands in the area before joining the army in 1942. The four years he spent in the services included spells in India, Burma and Singapore with the regimental band of the York and Lancaster Regiment.

After the war Burt became a pianist with the cabaret and revue act 'The Men About Town', and shortly afterwards he was offered his first TV engagement on *Kaleidoscope*. He wrote his first film score (*The Girl is Mine*) in 1950, during a period that saw him writing scores for most of the leading dance bands and radio orchestras.

He acted as musical director for various West End shows, and when the cabaret venue The Talk of the Town opened in London in the late 1950s he helped orchestrate the first revues there for Robert Nesbitt. In 1966 – by which time he had also worked extensively for the BBC – Burt became the venue's musical director, staying for sixteen years until its closure in 1982.

He scored and orchestrated the first James Bond movie, *Dr No*, as well as pieces for other films. As for his television career, Burt was the musical director for many programmes, including *The Benny Hill Show*, *The Lance Percival Show*, *Crackerjack* and *It's a Square World*.

and we didn't identify any of them. We'd both sit at pianos and work all day in the studio, simply calling them Tune A, Tune B, and so on. The tape was then handed to Ronnie Hazlehurst's secretary, who had the names of all the composers, and she in turn passed it on to John Howard Davies, who made the final choice.'

To Burt it was like winning the pools when the producer selected one of his titles. 'I'd submitted about three, and I didn't think much of the one he chose,' smiles Burt, who had first been given a brief regarding the style of programme. 'Sometimes the information you're given is a bit nebulous, but it gives you a feel for the type of show.'

CHOOSING COSTUMES

In charge of costume design for the first two series of *The Good Life* was Rita Reekie. When the scripts arrived on her desk, her first port of call was John Howard Davies' office. 'After reading the scripts, I met with the director and we talked through the project, discussing the characters and the jobs they had and forming a picture of the background of their lives, which helps point you in the right direction when it comes to costumes,' says Rita.

The next stage involved meeting the artists to hear their ideas about the characters. 'Obviously you tell them your views, and together decide how the character will dress.' As the costume designer, Rita would create a picture to inform the artist not just about style but form and colour, too. 'I'd guide them towards what I thought would work and, hopefully, everyone would agree. Out of all the discussions comes a character, who develops during the first series.'

Whenever an episode is repeated nowadays, part of the enjoyment is laughing at the fashions of the time, such as kipper ties, wide collars, flared trousers and long skirts in abundance. 'A lot of the clothes are hysterical, but they were fashionable at the time. I felt fortunate that long clothes were in evidence. You could wear a long frock while putting the rubbish

the first two series weren't as outrageous as in the final two, which was something I enjoyed introducing.'

As the character of Margo became increasingly dominant, her outfits reflected the shift. 'Although the clothes were more outrageous than before, it was important to keep something of the actor's own taste in the items chosen. If someone hates wearing blue, for example, you don't ever use that colour. But I tuned in to Penny very quickly and, to begin with, we would trot up to Harrods and buy most things there. After a while I got to know her sizes and would buy clothes and jewellery without her.'

out, and although it would be amusing, it was allowed because it was the fashion.'

Rita, who has worked mainly on drama productions, looks back on *The Good Life* as one of the best comedies she's been involved with, and she has great affection for the show. 'It was lovely. I did lots of drama, so the occasional sitcom provided light relief.'

Other commitments meant that she was unavailable for the final two series, so at that stage Sally Nieper, who had worked on the first series of *Last of the Summer Wine* and on *Monty Python's Flying Circus*, took over. The styles had already been set by the time Sally became involved, but she wanted to stamp her own mark on the costumes. 'Penny Keith's clothes in

From a costume designer's viewpoint, Margo (whose clothes used up most of the clothing budget) provided the biggest challenge, because her attire was flamboyant compared with her husband's formal look and the casual everyday style of the Goods. 'For Jerry, I'd go round with Paul to buy some suits and jackets. All I'd buy without him would be shirts, ties and sweaters, but when you got to know someone, it was easy buying for them,' says Sally, who turned to her own family when dressing Tom and Barbara.

'Most of the things they wore were items I'd gleaned off members of my family!' The clothes had to be well worn, so second-hand garments were ideal. 'In one episode Richard wore a green sweater with holes in it, which I'd knitted myself, while some of the little short-sleeved shirts Felicity wore had belonged to my husband in their former life.'

Sally Nieper, who left the BBC in 1979 to work freelance, remembers *The Good Life* as a happy show. 'We were all very close, like one big happy family. It was one of the best shows I ever worked on.'

MAKE-UP

In charge of make-up for series one, three and four and the Royal Command Performance was Marianne Ford. It was her first job after being promoted to

make-up supervisor. 'Being given *The Good Life* as the first show since my promotion was a wonderful beginning. Working with such professional people, who were all extremely generous towards each other, was great.'

After receiving the scripts, Marianne attended a meeting with John Howard Davies and other departmental representatives, during which budgets, characterizations, the cast and general expectations were on the agenda.

When the series went into production, one of her biggest challenges was continuity. 'Some scenes would be shot on location, then six weeks later they'd be in the studio doing the inside shots, so you had to

be on your toes. It was important to take the right continuity photographs so that you could match everything up.

'The only difficulty happens when, for example, you're shooting a long scene and a character flicks her hair from one side to the other. You've got to record everything that happens, so if bits have to be reshot you must know which side her hair was. That's when it can become complicated.'

When it comes to shooting outdoors, one of the worst enemies of continuity is fine drizzle, as Marianne explains. 'You get everybody set up and then it rains – but very fine, light rain that is invisible to the camera. During the 1970s flicked-up hair was in fashion, and it was one of the styles we used for Margo. If it was raining, you just had to hope that her hair wouldn't completely flop as the scene progressed, especially if it took several takes.'

Overall, the sitcom didn't present any major difficulties of this kind, and for Marianne – who worked on a variety of different productions, from Shakespeare to Ken Dodd – it turned out to be an uncomplicated project. 'I've worked on more challenging programmes during my career,' she remarks, 'but this was certainly one of the happiest.'

BEHIND THE CAMERA

Ken Willicombe, the film cameraman for the final two series, felt that one reason why the show became successful was that the actors were given freedom to express their feelings about the parts they were playing. 'It didn't seem to be a rigid script structure, and they were able to feed their views into the whole production.

'It was a good team, with John Howard Davies directing and Brian Jones able to organize it and keep the show under control. People can be very intense, though. If they're perfectionists they have their own standards to maintain, which can cause tension, but Brian was able to pacify everyone,' remarks Ken, who travelled the world for the BBC, beginning on documentaries and current affairs programmes such as *Whicker's World* and *Tonight*.

He appreciates that everyone has a vital role to play in a TV production, but feels the cameraman has a unique responsibility. 'We weren't using videos

at that point, so the poor old director didn't know until the following day what he'd actually got. It was important that the director got on with the cameraman, because it was through him that he expressed his ideas. I was there to interpret John Howard Davies' wishes photographically, producing the result he wanted while adding my own comments, and, in doing so, hopefully improving the overall effect.'

Taking over from Len Newson, who had been in charge of the camera for the first two series, was straightforward for Ken – who worked on many comedy shows, including *Porridge* and *The Dick Emery Show* – and he enjoyed working for John Howard Davies. 'He was excellent, and was always able to communicate exactly what he wanted from a particular shot.'

Considering the show's success, Ken – who spent 26 years at the BBC – believes it hit the screens at just the right moment, catching the tide of interest in self-sufficiency. 'My wife and I often talked about trying our hand at being more self-sufficient, and I remember having chats with Richard Briers about it in the pub. For us, we always thought it would be something to try when we retired, but now that we have, we realize it would be virtually impossible, maintaining a civilized lifestyle.' At their Somerset home the Willicombes grow produce as a hobby, from carrots and strawberries to their own vines for making home-made wine, but they gave up thoughts of total self-sufficiency long ago.

CREATING THE EFFECTS

Although *The Good Life* didn't require much in terms of visual effects, the special effects department was called upon occasionally during the sitcom's life. Peter Pegrum's work is credited in the closing titles for three episodes, but the experienced Tony Oxley was also assigned to the show from time to time, and it's he who can claim the plaudits for making the contraption Tom and Barbara passed off as a vehicle!

'It was made from an old tractor, a park seat and other bits and pieces, and took quite a lot of work,' recalls Tony, who was given the freedom to design the vehicle as he saw fit. 'I would have known from the script that a vehicle of some sort was required, and it was down to me to come up with something. It had to be fitted with explosions, puffs of smoke and different effects like that.'

After finding a clapped-out miniature tractor, he simply 'took bits off and stuck bits on'. 'It had to look as if it was made from realistic things, but in a way-out manner.' With the help of a park bench he made it into a two-seater, and after he'd fitted other oddments, the vehicle was ready for use. First seen in the episode 'A Tug of the Forelock', in the third series, his invention was used in a further three episodes.

Tony enjoyed working on the series. 'Everyone was good to work with, including all the actors. It was a show that worked well.'

TIME TO CALL IT A DAY

Our final chance to observe the lives of Tom and Barbara Good and their neighbours Margo and Jerry

Leadbetter was on 10 June 1978, with the screening of 'When I'm 65', the Royal Command Performance. But the fourth series had finished over a year earlier, with the foursome toasting the good life in 'Anniversary', one of the best, and most touching, of all the episodes – a view shared by many of the sitcom's fans.

The Audience Research Department at the BBC reported that 'the overwhelming majority of viewers found this final episode of *The Good Life* well up to the extremely high standards of the series.' In this episode the Goods return home one evening to find they've been burgled, which brings about a change of mood that some viewers found difficulty in

accepting. However, the majority's feeling was that 'the introduction of pathos enriched the comedy' and that 'indeed, this poignant – even shock – ending had great impact'.

The viewing sample were almost unanimous in their appreciation of the series. Such enthusiastic remarks as 'the best comedy series on TV', 'a spot of sheer delightful entertainment', 'with sharp original writing and excellent acting all round' and 'humour at its very, very best' were commonplace.

Praise for the actors was 'even more unreserved', according to the Audience Research Department, which had analysed 413 questionnaires completed by the viewing panel in response to 'Anniversary'. By now, some viewers were regarding Margo as the star of the show. The report's author wrote: 'There was a considerable feeling that Penelope Keith's characterization of Margo was outstanding and that the consequent change of focus from Tom and Barbara to Margo and her "perfect foil" Jerry was a natural development out of this "superb partnership".' However, it was felt that 'each of the characters was fully integral, each contributing importantly', and that 'the individual roles … were exceptionally well balanced, each complementing the other three, producing an effective contrast between the two couples. The portrayal of these characters was considered "brilliant" and "completely faultless".'

Bringing the final curtain down on the sitcom was the writers' own decision, and one Jimmy Gilbert respected. 'We'd done four series, and it's always up to the writers to say if they feel it's running out of steam and they want to leave while it's still on top. There was another way of doing it, which David Croft used to do occasionally, which was to take the show off but to keep it in the public's mind by recording the odd Christmas show, only to bring back another series later. But *The Good Life* had almost a serial element to it in the relationships and the seasons. And as it was such an individual series, if the writers felt that that was it, everybody would go along with them.'

After creating four series of *The Good Life*, the writers knew it was time to call it a day. 'We'd just run out of self-sufficiency stories,' admits Bob. 'We'd done pigs twice, chickens twice, the crops several times, and couldn't think of anything new. The show had become so popular that I think some of the actors were beginning to wonder whether we could keep up the standard – a justifiable fear.

'John and I knew that, if we carried on, the sitcom would be reduced to a series about two sets of neighbours. That would have worked, and we could probably have continued for another six years, it was so popular. But it wouldn't have been about self-sufficiency, which is where it started. So it was time to let go.'

FILE COPY

British Broadcasting Corporation

Confidential

AN AUDIENCE RESEARCH REPORT

(Week 21)

VR/77/29A

THE GOOD LIFE
by John Esmonde and Bob Larbey

Producer: John Howard Davies

Anniversary

Sunday 22nd May, 1977 8.05-8.35pm, BBC-1

1. Size and composition of audience (based on results of the survey of Listening and Viewing). It is estimated that the audience for this broadcast was 23.7% of the population of the United Kingdom. Programmes on BBC-2 and ITV at the time were seen by 0.4% (average over News on 2 and The Lively Arts : Berg) and 23.6% (The Royal Show).

The average audience for the seven programmes in this series was 25.7% of the population of the United Kingdom. The composition of the average audience (i.e. how it was divided in terms of age, sex, employment and social class) was as follows (for purposes of comparison an indication of the composition of the United Kingdom population is given in the right-hand column):-

	Average audience composition %	United Kingdom composition %
Age:-		
Children 5 – 14	18.6	16.3
15 – 19	7.9	8.1
20 – 29	14.9	14.8
30 – 49	25.7	27.4
50 +	32.9	33.4
All adults over 15	81.4	83.7
Total	100.0	100.0
Sex:-		
Boys under 15	8.3	8.3
Men (employed)	28.9	34.9
Men (not employed – mainly retired)	5.7	5.2
Total Males	42.9	48.4
Girls under 15	10.3	7.9
Women (employed)	18.6	17.4
Women (not employed – mainly h'wives)	28.2	26.3
Total Females	57.1	51.6
Total	100.0	100.0
Class:-		
Upper Middle	5.7	6.0
Lower Middle	37.5	24.0
Working	56.8	70.0
Total	100.0	100.0

Continued/..........

PULLING IN THE VIEWERS

Patience is a virtue – one that television executives need in large doses if they decide to gamble on a further series of a situation comedy. In today's TV climate the axe tends to be wielded far too quickly (although, with the quality of some of the sitcoms on offer nowadays, it's perhaps sometimes wise to put them out of their misery at an early stage). But even those with a reasonable chance of becoming successful as they mature are seldom given long enough to do so. Luckily, in the case of *The Good Life* the decision-makers spotted the potential in Esmonde and Larbey's suburban comedy, disregarded the lukewarm reception it received on its first run, and had sufficient faith in it to commission a further seven episodes. Their judgement was rewarded with one of the BBC's most popular shows, its audience figures peaking at 17.7 million for 'Whose Fleas are These?', the sixth episode in Series Three.

The audience figures grew as the series progressed:

Series	Average viewing figures
1	7.5 million
2	10.5 million
3	15.7 million
4	13.0 million*

* This series was let down by episode one, which attracted only 7.5 million viewers – perhaps as a result of the day of transmission being changed from a Friday to Sunday.

THE GOOD LIFE (Continued)

2. Reaction of audience (based on 413 questionnaires completed by 37% of the Viewing Panel).

The reactions of this sample of the audience were distributed as follows:-

A+ %	A %	B %	C %	C- %
35	52	12	1	0

giving a Reaction Index of 80, which compares favourably with the average of 75 for the rest of the series.

3. The overwhelming majority of reporting viewers found this final episode of The Good Life well up to the extremely high standard of the series. Although it was occasionally felt that the burglary brought an unsuitable change of mood and that consequently this episode was not as unified or as enjoyable as others, by far the greater number found that the introduction of pathos enriched the comedy and that, indeed, this quite poignant - even shock - ending had great impact; in all, possibly the best episode in the current series.

4. The series as a whole was, almost without exception, thought to be excellent: 'the best comedy series on T.V.', 'a spot of sheer delightful entertainment', 'humour at its very, very best!', with quite a number of viewers remarking that it couldn't be praised highly enough, and a very large number requesting a further series. One or two of the sample felt that it had become slightly tired and that some of the situations had become contrived but by far the overwhelming number felt that it was still very fresh and very different, 'a witty, adult comedy' that nevertheless could appeal to all ages ('no bad language or bad scenes'), 'with sharp original writing and excellent acting all round'.

5. Praise for the four main characters and their portrayal was even more unreserved and indeed it was often remarked that it was these extravagantly drawn but entirely believable four characters, far more than the sometimes unlikely stories built around them, which were the attraction. There was considerable feeling that Penelope Keith's characterisation of Margot was outstanding and the consequent change of focus from Tom & Barbara to Margot and her 'perfect foi Jerry was a natural development out of this 'superb partnership'; nevertheless it was felt that each of the characters was fully integral, each contributing importantly, and that the individual rôles (which, though clearly defined never approached the stereotyped) were exceptionally well-balanced, each perfectly complementing the other three, producing an effective contrast between the two couples. The portrayal of these characters was considered 'brilliant' and completely faultless.

6. 40% saw all seven episodes, 39% saw five or six, 14% three or four, 4% one or two and 3% were not sure.

Copyright of the BBC
AMC/MRS

Audience Research Department
13th July, 1977

'You just suddenly say, "Oh, that'll do," and leave the viewers wanting more – hopefully,' adds John Esmonde. 'It's nice when people react with disappointment when you tell them you're not doing any more, rather than saying "Thank God for that!". That's just what you don't want to hear. Overall, it was the right time to finish.'

When Bob and John announced their decision to the BBC, the response was indeed one of disappointment. 'They would have willingly gone for more,' says Bob, 'but I think everybody knew, deep down, that the time was right. It was best to get out on top, which we did.'

One person who agreed with Esmonde and Larbey's decision was the producer, John Howard Davies. 'Everyone connected with the show felt that four series was enough, because all that could happen now was for it to go down in quality. Anyway, I don't like doing long series, and *The Good Life* lasted longer than I'd normally have recommended. It's just that everything had gone so well. I don't think any of the episodes showed signs of tiredness, or that the standard of the scripts was slipping. We just felt that we'd done four series, a nice round figure in terms of calendar weeks and months, and that was enough.

'The writers anyway wanted to move on to other things, and so did the cast. The trouble for actors is that if you do several series of a programme over many years, there's a danger of getting typecast, and then everything you're asked to do thereafter is on the back of one thing you were successful in.'

LOOKING BACK

Many elements contributed to the sitcom's huge popularity: the fact that it was not only an original idea, dreamt up at just the right time for the British public, but had a glorious cast, the commitment shown by the BBC chiefs even when the first series failed to set the world alight, and the high quality of the scripts, to name just a few. Reflecting on the success of *The Good Life*, John Howard Davies stresses the importance of assembling the right cast. 'If you get the people you want, you're ninety per cent there. You can put all the right chemicals into the crucible, but if the catalyst isn't working properly you can still have a terrible failure on your hands.' John admits

there's a curious alchemy that sometimes comes into play, making everyone relaxed and happy and a given production successful. 'God knows what it is, but I wish *I* knew!'

Production Manager Brian Jones felt that the sitcom appealed to a large percentage of the public, many of whom were, like the Goods, having to watch their expenditure. 'A lot of people were having to tighten their belts, and the political temperature of the country at the time saw people looking at new ways of saving money. Combined with such a good set of actors, this helped make for a successful show.'

Another crucial factor in *The Good Life*'s success was the quality of the scripts, which were always of the highest order, as Jimmy Gilbert confirms. 'The scripts were absolutely superb, always based on the reality of the characters instead of just going for gags. Every one of the scripts was funny and real, and the characters were warm and believable, which is why the viewers grew to love the programme. It's a corny truism, but John and Bob are very honest in their scriptwriting. There's a great reality about their work, even though the situation is obviously pitched that bit higher than most people's idea of real life.'

Having to bring scripts alive can be a tough job for the director, but a good set of scripts from Esmonde and Larbey made John Howard Davies' task easier. 'The writing was excellent,' John comments. 'They

MY VIEW OF *THE GOOD LIFE*

by BBC executive producer GARETH GWENLAN

Although Gareth was not involved in the making of *The Good Life*, he had worked with the actors and is a fan of the series.

Esmonde and Larbey have always been good writers. The four characters in *The Good Life* were absolutely wonderful, well-rounded, multi-dimensional characters. And they were impeccably played by four of the best comedy actors we had: Dickie Briers, Felicity Kendal, Penny Keith and Paul Eddington. You won't find a much stronger team than that.

They each contributed, in their own way, to the success of the sitcom, and I think it was a wonderful show. It was just right for its time because there was a big interest in self-sufficiency, and what Esmonde and Larbey did was to grab that but place it in a suburban garden, populating it with those great characters. It's no wonder that whenever it's played it still does well. It's a classic and one that people will be watching in a hundred years and still enjoying. It was gentle, but perceptive and hugely enjoyable.

GOOD LIFE VIDEO & AUDIO CASSETTES

To date, two *Good Life* videos have been released in the UK and three in the States. Across the pond CBS Fox, in conjunction with the Beeb, released the first volume (catalogue no. 8498) in the spring of 1998. It features the episodes 'Backs to the Wall', 'The Windbreak War' and 'Silly, but it's Fun'. Later that year two further US volumes were issued. Volume Two (catalogue no. 0307) contains 'Pig's Lib', 'Just My Bill' and 'Mutiny', while Volume Three (catalogue no. 0308) offers 'Going to Pot', 'The Happy Event' and 'The Last Posh Frock'.

Back home, the BBC have served up two helpings of *The Good Life* on video. The first tape (catalogue no. BBCV5356), carrying the lead title 'Backs to the Wall', was released in October 1994 (price £10.99) and, in common with its later US counterpart, also contained the episodes 'The Windbreak War' and 'Silly, but it's Fun'. An earlier release – a WHS Exclusive (catalogue no. WHS4437) issued in January 1992 but since deleted from the list – contained the first two episodes, 'Plough Your Own Furrow' and 'Say Little Hen…'.

A BBC audio cassette (catalogue no. BBC 0563381183) is also available. Released in May 1997, it features the four episodes 'Plough Your Own Furrow', 'The Thing in the Cellar', 'The Pagan Rite' and 'The Guru of Surbiton'.

produced the type of script one gets very occasionally in life, where you don't have to alter anything. They're very professional writers. Luckily for everyone concerned, the BBC had faith in the show, and even though the first series pulled in only a low audience, a second and third series were sanctioned to establish it. The audiences were terrible for the first series and

only picked up slightly for the second. It wasn't until the third that we really hit the big time.'

Sadly, such loyalty is rarely shown towards new sitcoms in today's tough market. If a programme fails to attract a sizeable audience at the first attempt, it's banished from the screen and left to rot in the TV station's vaults. John Howard Davies believes that the fear of failure lies behind this somewhat shortsighted approach. 'Commercial companies obviously have a different priority. They've got to deliver an audience to the advertiser, and if they don't, the show's off. But that puts an enormous strain on any new comedy, because it won't always work the first time around.'

But with *The Good Life* he knew there was a future. 'You can sense when you're working on something good. You may not know how good, but I had faith in the show.' Many people class this self-sufficiency comedy as one of the BBC's top sitcoms, but John Howard Davies finds it hard to rate it in those terms. 'Some people describe it as "lovely" or "ever so sweet", but there are better programmes and there are worse ones, so you can't say it was one of the best or worst. All you can safely say is that it was very successful in its time. Comedy is so subjective, anyway,' he adds.

3. Over three-quarters of the sample continued to be amused by this 'refreshing' and 'topical' comedy centring on the efforts of the likeable Good couple to be self-sufficient in Surbiton - in this edition, suffering invasion by a couple of trendy hippies. 'Hilarious' moments clearly resulted from 'well observed', if exaggerated, characters and situations; especially from the contrast between the Goods and the neighbouring Leadbeatters, 'very much Surbiton' - the wife, Margo, being afforded some 'good opportunities' for comment by the hippies' arrival. Altogether it seems this was most enjoyable 'clean' family comedy - for one in every five reporting viewers, 'brilliant', even.

4. Though a sizeable group reacted with moderate appreciation of an 'inconsequential but entertaining' programme, there was little strong criticism, apart from a few who were slightly bored with the 'feeble story' and rather 'stock characters' in some instances remarking that the novelty had 'worn off a little'.

5. 'Easy and stylish', the performance was keenly applauded by most of the sample, who evidently found the couples well-matched in themselves and excellent foils for each other; Penelope Keith as the smart Margo was perhaps a particularly memorable portrait. In a generally good production, sets and clothes which aptly highlighted the different life-styles were commended.

---

3. Reporting viewers were usually delighted to welcome this very popular series back on their screens and, if a few did not consider The Early Birds one of the best episodes they'd seen, the great majority thoroughly enjoyed it. The plot (which revolved round Tom and Barbara's decision to get up and go to bed with the sun, regardless of what the clocks said) was good, but this was really of secondary importance, viewers thought, the main attraction lying, as always, in the characters themselves - Tom and Barbara, the enthusiastic, idealistic, rather touching self-sufficiency 'nuts' and the ultra-sophisticated Margo and Jerry, whose half-affectionate, half-exasperated relationship with their unconventional next-door neighbours provided much of the fun. The humour was refreshing, the characters likeable, it was agreed, and the performance throughout was extremely good, Richard Briers and Felicity Kendal being delightfully natural as the Goods and Paul Eddington and Penelope Keith excelling as their neighbours ('absolute treasures, both of them') - indeed, several felt that Miss Keith almost stole the show with her portrayal of Margo, the 'grand-dame' of Surbiton.

4. 94% of the sample watched the whole programme, 4% came in in the middle and 2% either tried a bit or switched off before the end.

3. 'Funny but feasible', the comedy of relationships between the self-sufficient Goods and the neighbouring, conventionally suburban Leadbeatters continued to delight most of those reporting - with many of whom the series had clearly become an established favourite.

4. A few members of the sample said they had not enjoyed this week's edition as much as usual, sometimes adding that they had found it a little slow and lacking in action. However, stray critics were greatly outnumbered by those who were most amused by a programme which they found well up to the usual standard of the series. Characters who were recognisable although exaggerated, and on the whole very likeable, and credible dialogue contributed to the appeal of the situation when the Goods decided to talk to their plants to encourage them to grow (a practice in which, from the comments of some of those reporting, it seems they are not alone) and Margo Leadbeat held a musical reunion.

5. Occasionally reporting viewers commented on Felicity Kendal's hoarse voice or asked whether she had a cold but on the whole, there was warm praise for the 'superb comedy performance' of an excellent cast who complemented each other extremely well - though for several viewers Penelope Keith as Margo rather stole the show. There was equally keen approval of a production in which attention to detail contributed to a general feeling of authenticity and helped bring out the differences between the two households - Margo's smart clothes and 'fab' house being particularly mentioned.

SUNDAY
17th
APRIL
1977

3. The enjoyment and entertainment provided by previous series of The Good Life was the over-riding reason for viewers watching this episode, which was the second in the new series. This, together with the fact that it is widely regarded as 'ideal family viewing' as well as 'humorous and refreshing', maintains its position as one of the most highly regarded comedy shows currently on the air.

4. The minor reservation that the plot of this particular episode was not as strong as some of the earlier ones was more than compensated for by the excellence of the acting of the four main characters, it was thought, and although Felicity Kendal and Richard Briers were sometimes accused of over-acting this was denied by the large number who thought that all the members of the cast were ideally suited to their parts. Penelope Keith was singled out for particular praise (indeed a number of panel members gave her as their reason for watching the show), but generally everyone agreed that together they make a fine team and a first class show. The production too was highly thought of, as the use of film and the two contrasting house sets lent a great deal of realism to the programme.

MONDAY
26th
DECEMBER
1977

3. The overwhelming majority of reporting viewers found this special Christmas edition of The Good Life hugely enjoyable. It was generally considered to be a superbly funny situation comedy with excellent dialogue and repartee, and this particular story-line, it was agreed, had been very strong, with a good twist at the end together with an appropriate seasonal atmosphere. One or two did think the programme somewhat predictable but they were most decidedly in a minority for nearly all found this a most enjoyable and entertaining show.

4. The performances given by the four main characters in the cast (Richard Briers, Penelope Keith, Felicity Kendal and Paul Eddington) were universally praised. It was felt that they made an excellent team, were brilliantly cast and portrayed. It was agreed that they were all amusing in their various ways and were very natural and convincing ('the whole cast seem so natural together that one doesn't realize they are acting at all'). Indeed, it was agreed by many that this show boasted the best acting in any television comedy series at present being shown.

5. The production, like the rest of the programme, was highly praised ('as always excellent'). Sets, lighting, camera-work and costumes were considered to be of a high standard, and it was agreed that the programme was very well thought out and produced; indeed, the whole programme was considered altogether excellent.

Although he hasn't himself seen the show for several years (so wouldn't like to comment on whether it has stood the test of time), John feels that the concept and the fashions are the elements that would date, '…but that's part of the sitcom's charm'.

Jimmy Gilbert hasn't caught an episode for some time either, but he feels the show would still appeal to viewers today. 'Most comedy series date, although there are always exceptions to the rule, like *Fawlty Towers*. But I would have thought people would still be interested in the relationships in *The Good Life*.'

The humour that emanates from Esmonde and Larbey's scripts is inoffensive, unthreatening and warming. As G. Stoodley Thomas wrote in the *Western Mail* in 1989, viewers looked to the genre of situation comedy for 'easy, pleasant shows, demanding no

mental ability to follow them, near enough to real life – but not too near – and including characters or stock types with whom they can identify, and situations in which they might just possibly find themselves. Cosy viewing, in fact.'

The Good Life was just that, and Bob Larbey feels it's typical of his and Esmonde's style of writing. 'Gentle is a word often applied to our writing, which is sometimes another way of saying it's not very funny. When people, including critics, talk about "gentle comedy", that generally means there are not a lot of laughs but it's quite nice. We never intended to write "gentle" comedies, it just became our style.'

Writing in a manner that didn't offend was the kind of humour Bob respected. 'It's what we like. It never occurred to us to attack anything as a lot of

comedies have done – sometimes very successfully, too.' Some critics and academics try tagging their sitcoms with a host of inner meanings, or dreaming up underlying themes that are expressed, perhaps tacitly, through their work. 'With *Please, Sir!* a lot of people thought it was some sort of social document, that we were making a serious statement about the educational system. If we were, it was very understated! It wasn't something we'd set out to do, we just wrote the truth as we saw it – if fiction *can* be the truth.'

At the outset no one had an inkling of the success *The Good Life* would achieve, not even the writers. 'It's not that we thought it was going to be awful, it's just that you never really know. When a show begins to take off, you wise up to the fact pretty quickly, but let's face it, if you knew what the magic ingredients for success were, you'd always come up with a winner.

We simply hoped it would work, and luckily for us, and many other people, it did.'

Bob Larbey feels that, by the second series, he knew it was catching on. 'It started with five million, which was tiny in those days, and the reviews were mixed, so there was nothing good about it at all. The BBC stuck by it and commissioned a second series, and by episode two or three it had begun taking off, with the press suddenly loving it.' Not that this surprises Bob. 'I always thought of me and John as slow burners. We didn't write the kind of stuff that hit instantly, and *The Good Life* certainly didn't.'

Looking back over their illustrious writing career, the writers are rightfully proud of *The Good Life*. 'I'm proud of the fact that it was *about* something,' explains John. 'It was of its time, and technically its production was good enough. When I watch an

episode now, I don't cringe at the technicalities of it. Obviously, there's the odd line where I think, "Crikey, I wish I hadn't written that," but the rest is fine. And although some parts of it have become dated, like the talk of money, that makes it interesting, almost like a historical document.' Of all their catalogue of sitcoms, *The Good Life* has been the biggest earner over the years. 'It's always playing somewhere in the world, and on stations like UK Gold. It's been repeated on the BBC about three times already and, who knows, it might be again.'

THE SPIN-OFFS

T*he Good Life* has been shown around the globe. In America it was first transmitted by PBS in 1985, but had to be retitled. In August 1971 NBC had shown the first episode of a US sitcom called *The Good Life*, starring Larry Hagman (alias J.R. Ewing of *Dallas*). To avoid confusion, the name of Esmonde and Larbey's show was changed to *Good Neighbors*. After the sitcom's initial run on PBS, it wasn't seen again until CBS Fox released the first of three videos in 1998.

'The show has never been networked, but it still plays and we continue to get cheques from single stations throughout the US. Quite a lot of people know of it, which is pleasing,' says Bob Larbey. At one stage he and John Esmonde were involved in negotiations regarding a US adaptation of the show. 'There had been talk of an American version for about fifteen years. The last time we were in Los Angeles, about eight years ago, somebody was thinking of doing it. After we finished our meeting with this team of about fifty people, the chief announced, "We all have a similar thought here. Is there a way of doing it without the self-sufficiency?" That has to be one of the greatest quotes I've ever heard. He even added, "Couldn't Tom be a watchmaker, or something like that?" So no, it never happened – which is hardly surprising!'

Unlike other sitcoms, there were never any plans to make a movie of *The Good Life*. 'If there was talk, nothing ever came of it,' says Bob. 'I don't think it would have worked anyway. Most of the films made of a TV series involve everyone going off on holiday, or something like that, but with *The Good Life* you couldn't have the characters doing anything else. So we never got a call from Hollywood.'

THE WRITERS

JOHN ESMONDE

Even as a boy, John Esmonde knew that he wanted to be his own boss one day, preferably in the entertainment world. Since he came from a long line of musicians and singers, it would not have surprised anyone if he had pursued a musical career, but John is quick to point out that he lacked sufficient talent in that direction. 'Music has always interested me, and I do play the piano and sing. But I soon learnt what level you have to reach to turn professional, and I definitely wasn't that good.' His grandmother, however, was. 'She made singing, especially opera, her living. And my mother and brother were good, too, although they weren't professionals.'

Born in Battersea, London, in 1937, John – whose father was a buyer for a local industry – was educated at the Henry Thornton School in Clapham, the same grammar school that Bob Larbey went to, although he was three years ahead of John. Their friendship began during a school trip to Switzerland. 'We had a great time, probably because we discovered we were both loonies,' he admits with a smile. 'We had lots in common, including a crass schoolboy humour.'

John left school, where he had excelled in sport, and served his national service in the RAF, finishing up working on air ambulances. On his return to 'civvy street' he took an office job with a paint company, but it was not long before he joined the magazine business, where he was given the chance to write professionally. 'I became a journalist, initially on medical journals, before drifting into technical journalism, writing about food processing and packaging, that sort of thing.'

His friendship with Bob Larbey continued beyond the classroom, and they met frequently for lunch. During these get-togethers they would idle away the time by discussing how much they hated their jobs and wishing they could do something else with their lives. Other favourite topics were local revues and their favourite radio shows. Eventually the pair plucked up enough courage to try writing some sketches themselves, and before long they had sold their first piece of comedy writing. John and Bob knew they had found their niche in life, and this marked the beginning of two glittering careers,

during which they co-wrote more than sixteen hit TV shows.

John now lives in Spain, where he's enjoying his retirement after a long and successful career. 'Granada is a lovely place, and from our house we can look out onto the Mediterranean – it's wonderful.' But John still writes, although he concentrates on novels now. 'I haven't had one published yet, but being rejected makes me feel young again! I remember Bob and I used to send out sketches by the ton in the early days. And they came back by the ton, with notes stating bluntly: "We do not accept unsolicited material." That's one of the famous phrases.'

To date, John has completed two novels and enough short stories for a couple of books. 'One of the short story books has the working title "PC Tales" as it's all about computers. Machines frighten me, I hate them. But I must admit, I've become addicted to my computer, though it's taken some time.'

BOB LARBEY

It was some years before Bob Larbey had any inkling of what he wanted to do with his life. Since he enjoyed sport and English at school, he thought it must be wonderful earning a living writing about sport, but with the prospect of two years' national service looming, he remained undecided. 'You'd leave school at eighteen with A-levels and go straight into the forces, so if you were unsure about your future beforehand, you certainly weren't helped knowing it would be another two years until you could do anything about it.'

Bob was born in Clapham, South London, in 1934. His father spent his life working in the theatre, initially as a stage carpenter. 'He loved the theatre and enjoyed nothing more than talking about it. He tried his luck at acting, spending some time with a touring company, but when his children came along, reality reared its head and he returned to his trade to earn regular money.'

Bob enjoyed his schooldays. 'The older I got, the more I liked school, which I think is how a lot of people feel. The first and second forms were murder, but by the time you reach the fifth and sixth form you're treated like real people.' While he performed well in sports and English, mathematics was a different matter. 'When I took my mock exams, I only got eight per cent. I remember saying to the teacher, "Do you know, sir, I think it's about time I dropped maths." He replied solemnly, "I think it is, Larbey." A huge relief was felt by all!'

From 1952 to 1954 Bob served with the army's Middlesex Regiment, based in North London. But he spent most of his military days in Germany. 'Because I had a couple of A-levels they put me in the education corps, thinking I must be one of the clever buggers. It was a laugh, though, and quite a cushy life.'

After demob it was time for Bob to give serious consideration to his future, but he was still unsure what he wanted to do. 'So I went and worked for a printing block maker. It was an office job and extremely boring. John and I both wallowed for a few years, doing very little except moan about work.

'From my point of view, I knew I wasn't going to be any good at it. I'm not dumb, but I'm no business type, either,' says Bob. 'It began to dawn on me that I'd never be a captain of industry, I didn't have whatever it took. If I'd stayed I would have simply jogged along until it was time to claim my retirement clock.'

Fortunately for Bob and John, their writing partnership became so successful that in due course they were able to leave the world of printing blocks and food processing behind. After achieving success on the radio, they progressed to the small screen, quickly establishing themselves as one of Britain's foremost scriptwriting partnerships.

But Bob has also been successful writing on his own, as proven by *A Fine Romance* (1981–4), with Judi Dench and Michael Williams, and *As Time Goes By* (1992–), starring Judi Dench, again, and Geoffrey Palmer.

A Fine Romance was the first sitcom Bob wrote without his professional partner. 'It was a weird feeling.

Although it was quiet, I missed having someone to talk to about ideas. On the other hand, there was no other opinion to consider – only my own. There was no one to say "Is that *really* funny?" or "Would they *really* do that?" But it took some getting used to.'

Bob also faced the worry of whether he could succeed alone, as he'd never tried before. Would he be able to produce something worthy on his own? He had to find out, because he needed to maintain payments on a bridging loan. 'We'd just moved to our house near Capel, in Surrey – which cost us £50,000, a fortune in those days and as much as I could afford. But we couldn't sell our house in London so we had to take out a bridging loan, with interest rates at

WHO COMES FIRST?

Writing with a partner means that you have to decide whose name to use first. Should it be Esmonde & Larbey or Larbey & Esmonde? For John and Bob, a simple flick of a coin solved the dilemma. John won the toss, and that was that. As Bob points out, 'We didn't go into any debate about it, it simply didn't matter that much.'

17 per cent. It was tough, and just when John and I had talked about cutting back on working together.

'Things were going well. We were making money and life was pretty secure, but John wanted to spend more time in Spain. He said, "I don't really want to work all through the summer. It's silly having a fortnight off as though we're still at work. Let's have three months off." I agreed with him, but then came the bridging loan, and things got tight.'

Bob phoned his agent, explaining his predicament. 'She laughed and asked, "What do you intend doing? Are you going to go out minicabbing?" I told her I would if necessary, to which she responded, "I'll just remind you that you're a comedy writer, so why don't you write a comedy?" That made sense, so I sat down at home and wrote *A Fine Romance*.'

Bob took the first script to Humphrey Barclay at LWT, who commissioned the first of four series, and the sitcom soon took off. 'Having Judi Dench in it didn't hurt!' laughs Bob, who remembers being involved in discussions regarding casting. 'Humphrey and I were bandying names about for the female lead and he said, "Look, we're going backwards and forwards here. In an ideal world, who would you like to play Laura?" I told him Judi Dench, and he replied, "Why not?" I told him Judi didn't do television comedy, but he said that didn't prevent us from sending her a script. And blow me, a week later he told me, "She laughed like a drain. She wants to do it." I was in a daze for about three weeks. I just couldn't believe my luck.'

Bob Larbey, who still lives in Surrey, continues to write and has a new series of *As Time Goes By* in the pipeline.

THINKING ALONG THE SAME LINES...

John Esmonde and Bob Larbey floated the idea of trying their luck as professional writers over a plate of egg and chips at a Wimpy restaurant in London. 'We did a lot of moaning,' admits Bob. 'There were plenty of "Oh Gods" and "there must be something better than this". Neither of us liked our job, and there was certainly no job satisfaction. We were itching to do something about it, but what?' Another regular topic of conversation, when they weren't grumbling about work, was West End revue, something they both enjoyed. 'We caught the tail-end of the revue scene, and loved watching people like Kenneth Williams and Dora Bryan.'

The sketches that made them both laugh provided the much-needed spark to launch their careers as professional writers. 'I don't know whose idea it was, but one of us suggested we try writing sketches like some of the ones we'd seen,' Bob recalls. 'They were only two or three minutes long, and we were always dreaming up ideas to make each other laugh. From all the programmes we'd bought we knew that a lot of writers contributed to a revue, so we wondered whether we could as well.'

For the first time John and Bob could see a little chink of light in the gloom surrounding their dead-end jobs. Eager to try their luck, they met at John's house in the evenings after work, which was only a quarter of a mile from where Bob lived in Battersea. They started out writing short sketches, but, realizing that the era of revue was passing, soon turned their attention to radio. Bob explains: 'Radio seemed the obvious market. It was the early 1960s and there was still a lot of comedy on the radio, so we bombarded producers with our material.' Their style of work, in

those early days, was offbeat. 'The sketches tended to be on the manic side,' smiles Bob. 'There was no social realism or anything like that, we'd just put anything down that seemed a bit wild or slightly peculiar.'

Like most aspiring writers, Bob and John found it hard forcing their way into the highly competitive market of comedy writing, with rejection letters slipping through their letterboxes at an alarming rate. In hindsight, John Esmonde feels that their lack of strategy was a contributory factor. 'We made the mistake of blanket bombing, as opposed to pinpoint targeting. Then we got an agent, who taught us that instead of throwing tons of material at a producer, you've got to be more specific.'

From the very beginning of their writing relationship, Bob and John found working together easy. 'From the time we met at school, we've always had the same sense of humour,' says Bob. 'We made each other laugh, and on good days found we could make others laugh, too. I think a shared sense of humour is often the basis of a good friendship, and I can't imagine working with anyone who didn't appreciate the same humour as me. It would be very depressing.'

John Esmonde agrees. 'We didn't have to explain things to each other, it was almost as if we had a telepathic sense.' And they were never precious with each other. If either of them disliked a particular line, he would say so. They wouldn't waste time beating about the bush, worrying about hurting the other's feelings – they knew each other too well for that.

If you have the required talent, persistence eventually pays off. It did so in John and Bob's case and in due course they sold their first sketch, although they can't now remember to which radio programme. 'It was a show with Cyril Fletcher, and we managed to sell a two-line sketch,' recalls Bob. 'It was about an old chap and old girl talking to each other. He said something like "I love you desperately, Gladys, but we can never become man and wife," and when she asked why he replied, "Because I'm a mod and you're a rocker." We were paid two guineas for that.'

Gradually they sold more and more sketches, earning anything from three to ten guineas a time. Then they broke into television, supplying sketches for *The Dick Emery Show*, which began its eighteen-year run in 1963. Acting on their agent's earlier advice, John and Bob adapted their style of writing to the prospective market, increasing their success rate in the process. 'We listened to the shows we were submitting material to and got a feel for the kind of thing they used,' explains Bob. 'For Dick Emery, a man of many voices and characters, it was all about thinking of a character he'd enjoy playing, then you were away.'

Hit radio shows like *Beyond Our Ken* and *Round the Horne* were key influences in Esmonde and Larbey's early years. 'We also liked Jerry Lewis,' says John. 'I've always enjoyed surreal things, so anything along those lines got through to me.'

Eclipsing the pleasure of actually receiving money for their sketches was the sense of exhilaration they got from hearing professional actors uttering their lines on the radio. 'It was enormously exciting,' enthuses Bob. 'And of course it helps, hearing someone say your words. We obviously read them out to each other beforehand, but nothing beats hearing your lines coming out of a professional's mouth. It was extraordinary.'

For the first three years of their partnership, the pair fitted their creative work in around the day jobs, but, as their writing careers prospered, they reached a crucial stage in their lives. 'We started getting enough positive feedback to make us wonder whether we were good enough to write full-time, as producers were asking to see anything else we'd done,' says Bob. 'So that was all bubbling away, and in the meantime we were falling asleep at work because we were getting so physically tired – all the work was taking its toll.'

After an encouraging conversation with Edward Taylor, a radio producer at the BBC, John and Bob finally gambled with their futures by quitting their regular jobs and taking up writing on a full-time basis. 'We had an idea for some sketches and got talking to Ted Taylor, who was wonderful, one of our early mentors,' recalls Bob Larbey. 'He suggested, "You should have a go at something a bit longer than sketches. Have you ever thought of writing a half-hour?" We hadn't, but said we'd give it a try.'

It wasn't long before they were commissioned to write their first series for radio, *Spare a Copper*, on the strength of which they hoped to be able to go on writing for a living and make some money out of it. 'We were offered something like eighty guineas an episode, and thought we'd really made it,' says Bob, who admits it wasn't easy resigning from their jobs. 'It was a bigger decision for John because he was married, with even more responsibilities than me.'

'One reason for my success is that I have a very understanding wife, who was prepared to support me in those early days,' says John. 'She was one hundred per cent behind me.' But his wife's support was severely tested early on, when money was tight and opportunities scarce, and there were times when she had to take over as the couple's main breadwinner. 'She worked as a sales rep, selling books to people in offices as well as door-to-door. It was a hard slog, but we had to eat.'

John and Bob describe their days as novice writers as 'absolutely terrifying'. 'In one way, we were full of elation because we were actually doing something we'd wanted to do for ages,' but there was also the realization that nobody was going to just hand us a pay packet at the end of each week,' says Bob. 'It was down to us to earn it.'

But they knew it was something they had to try. 'I was about 32 and John 30, so it was really a case of now or never. We had to give it our full whack, or just forget the whole idea of becoming writers. If we hadn't left work then, we'd never have done it. We would just have ponced about on the outskirts writing sketches all the time. But instead we worked out how much we needed to live on and went for it.'

The first series of *Spare a Copper*, which consisted of six instalments and starred Kenneth Connor as PC Albert Hereward Lamp and Deryck Guyler as the police sergeant, was broadcast on 27 August 1965, in the same year that John and Bob turned professional. Everything was riding on a second series being commissioned, and mercifully it was, with the first of nine episodes going out on 13 June 1966. Bob Larbey was pleased with their first success. 'It didn't work badly, and we realized that, when it came to half-hour programmes, we couldn't rely on the manic stuff we had in sketches. We knew we weren't going to be the funniest writers in the world, but we enjoyed writing character comedy, which is what sitcom is all about.'

John and Bob were honing their skills for the genre that would eventually make them leading figures in the world of television. The success stories in situation comedy tend to be shows that depend on character study instead of a torrent of gags every week. 'If you get the characters right, it'll work,' claims Bob. 'Gag comedy is very hit-or-miss – if it works, it's funny, but if it doesn't, just forget it. If you've got characters that the audience can become interested in, or empathize with, you've established a bedrock. People start to care, and that's what our early radio work taught us. We weren't going to write material that would receive gales of laughter all the way through, but people would become fond of our characters.'

Both writers believe they owe a debt of gratitude to Edward Taylor, who produced *Spare a Copper*, for

BRIERS ON ESMONDE & LARBEY

Bob and John have a rare instinct for comedy, but they're capable of writing touching dramatic scenes, too. They dreamt up the episode 'Anniversary', in which the Goods' place was vandalized. It was a great episode, and when it came to recording it there was a huge curtain right across the studio, so that the audience couldn't see the set. When it was drawn aside, everyone went 'Ahhh!'. They loved us all so much, they couldn't bear it. It was a very dramatic episode – we went straight that week.

What I most like about John and Bob's writing is that they create real characters. When I played Martin in *Ever Decreasing Circles* they told me they'd based the character on a bloke they saw refereeing a football match on Clapham Common. He was being terribly vicious and pushy, blowing his whistle all the time, often for no real reason. When the match ended, everyone glared at him and rushed off to have a drink, leaving this bloke saying, 'Hey, boys, where are you going?' All they wanted to do was get him out of their sight. That was the influence behind Martin, and they created a character that people identified with. Everyone could recognize a little bit of Martin Bryce in someone they knew.

Some writers feel they need to induce a laugh every other line, which in my view isn't sitcom. Once you establish the storyline and get involved in the characters, the audience will laugh anyway. Bob and John always humanized their characters, and people warmed to them. Quite simply, they are great comedy writers.

the help and guidance he gave them during those early days. 'When we'd written the scripts, the three of us would sit down and read them through,' says Bob. 'We'd play all the characters and make little alterations. He was enormously helpful, not by coming up with any cracking lines, but in terms of sheer experience. He gave endless advice, and we were very grateful.'

Now that Esmonde and Larbey were writing for a living, the pressure was on for them to produce a constant supply of saleable material. The financial cushion provided by their previous salaries no longer existed, so for both of them the ability to pay regular bills was wholly dependent on selling their work. This worry never dampened their enthusiasm, but it wasn't until the second series of *Spare a Copper* was sanctioned that they felt confident they could really make a living out of writing. 'When the first series ended and we were sweating to find out whether there'd be a second, there was a period when we thought, "Oh God, has this all gone terribly wrong? Will we have to start our lives all over again?" But when we got the second series, we felt much more confident about the future.'

As professionals, it was important for them to establish an environment conducive to writing saleable material, but until they could afford to rent their own office, a box room at the top of the staircase in John Esmonde's Wimbledon home had to suffice. 'We never started work early, because we're totally useless first thing in the morning,' smiles Bob. 'We'd start about eleven and work through until six, maybe longer if we were on a roll, or something was urgent. That suited both our body clocks.'

'We used to sit in this little room and do these funny voices to each other,' says John. They also learnt how to construct a synopsis and handle the different technicalities of writing for radio and television. 'We learnt how to write for effects, or camera movements, that sort of thing. But we never went overboard, because that can upset directors terribly. You don't want to keep telling them what they're supposed to be doing.'

Working from home can also have its downside, as Bob Larbey explains. 'The only setback is when there's a cricket match on TV and you find yourself saying, "We'll just watch two overs." You have to be very disciplined.'

Unlike other successful writing partnerships, Bob and John's tasks weren't allocated on their individual strengths – responsibilities were simply split down the middle. 'I can't really say one of us had any particular speciality,' admits John, 'we just shared the work out. We used to write longhand, as opposed to typing the script or putting it onto computer straight away, which we always found distracting. When we were creating a script, we'd take it in turns to do the writing while we played all the characters out very badly, but to our ears they were perfect.'

'Mostly, we'd get into a stream of improvised dialogue and afterwards try and remember what it was that had made us laugh, then write it down. But we never adopted particular roles, with each of us always doing a set job,' recalls Bob, who is keen to stress that they never experienced any problems. 'I could never imagine writing with anyone else but John. The success we enjoyed together is partly due to having known each other for so long. Having been friends first made writing more of a shared pleasure.' Although they usually see eye to eye, an agreement was reached early on to prevent disagreements, as Bob explains. 'We had a cut-off point. If we were arguing about something, such as a line of dialogue, and one of us felt strongly that it shouldn't be in the script, then the line went. We disagreed very little, but if we did, we'd simply shrug and move on.'

For most projects, Esmonde and Larbey would write out a detailed overview, breaking episodes down scene by scene. While they found writing scripts fairly straightforward, the hardest part of the entire process was finding a different story for each episode. They were still cutting their teeth in terms of professional writing and gratefully accepted any advice going. As John recalls, fellow writers Barry Took and Marty Feldman offered plenty of help. 'They took time to positively criticize our work. We'd go in and see them, and they'd say things like, "Don't you think that's a bit obvious?" or "That's been done before." They were prepared to sit down and advise us, which we appreciated.'

After the success of *Spare a Copper* on radio, John and Bob fancied trying their hand at a sitcom for TV.

As well as broadening their overall experience, small screen success would bring financial rewards, too. 'It's a lot more money, and you have to think in those terms if you're going to be a pro,' says John Esmonde. 'It's nothing to be ashamed of. If you're a professional writer, then that's what it's all about.'

Moving on to television is a natural progression for any scriptwriter. 'Being a different form of writing, it provides a fresh opportunity,' says John. 'It's amazing what you can do with a shot on camera, and television makes you more economic with dialogue. On radio you have to tell the listeners everything, or at least suggest everything.' Luckily, they found the transition relatively painless. 'It was very pleasant knowing we could write successfully for TV as well.'

They had already written for television in the form of comedy sketches for the likes of Dick Emery, but their first stab at situation comedy came in the shape of *Room at the Bottom* in 1966. Transmitted as part of the long-running *Comedy Playhouse*, a series was commissioned on the strength of the pilot, and a year later seven episodes were screened, starring Kenneth Connor as Gus Fogg and Deryck Guyler as Mr Powell. The sitcom focused on the lives of maintenance men working at a manufacturing company, led by Connor. When the series was requested, it made for exciting times. 'It was like the best thing that had ever happened in the entire world,' enthuses Bob Larbey, who remembers sitting down to watch the pilot being transmitted, all those years ago. 'It was very nail-biting! I think I was probably too nervous to laugh.'

The sitcom was conceived after the writers considered who actually ran many of the industries springing up all over the capital. 'We used to keep passing all these big buildings along Millbank, on the edge of the Thames, and asked ourselves the question, "Who really runs places like that?" We decided it was the maintenance men in a room at the bottom who controlled the whole thing – and that's what the sitcom was about,' explains Bob. 'The maintenance men in our show were always on the fiddle, and were drawing wages for somebody who'd been dead for about fifteen years!' When a new broom arrives and becomes suspicious, he asks the maintenance men to produce the man, and that's when the fun begins.

Although *Room at the Bottom* never made it beyond the first series, the writers were pleased with their baptism into the world of TV sitcom. 'It worked well, and was quite a good little story,' says Bob, who admits, nevertheless, that they still had a lot to learn at that stage. 'Even though I liked it, I don't think it was written well enough. With people like Kenneth Connor and Deryck Guyler we had extremely expert performers, and the fact that it didn't go to a second series was no reflection at all on their performance.'

John Esmonde admits that the sitcom's transmission was not a 'world-stopping event', but he thought it a good idea. 'I was pleased with it, and it isn't one of those things that makes me shudder with shame when I look back on it. But so much depends on what mood the viewers are in as to whether a show takes off or not.'

With an entire TV series under their belt, it was time for Esmonde and Larbey to move out of John's box room and find an office to work in. 'Once we started in television we became more serious, and more financially secure,' remarks Bob. 'We realized we couldn't carry on saying "Let's just watch two overs and see what the score is" every time there was a cricket match on the telly. We needed somewhere neutral.'

Another reason for finding an office was John Esmonde's move to Ferring, on the Sussex coast. Looking for a site roughly halfway between their respective homes, they found a little room in Dorking, which became their first office. But their chosen location was far from palatial. 'It was a strange sort of building with lots of little offices, one occupied by a photographer and another by someone who made pills of some sort,' recalls Bob.

Although they could see the hills beyond Dorking in the distance, their office overlooked the car park. It wasn't the most uplifting of locations, but just the ticket for two writers who wanted to rid themselves of any possible distractions. John explains, 'We didn't want glamorous offices with a fantastic view. If we were sitting around on swanky armchairs admiring the landscape, it wouldn't be conducive to work, whereas if your surroundings are basic – and I do mean basic – you get on with things.'

'We quickly turned the place into a slum, as writers usually do,' laughs Bob. 'It wasn't long before there was fag-ash, cups that hadn't been washed for days and bits of paper everywhere.' These conditions shocked their visitors. 'Not many people came to our office, but those who did used to say, "Oh my God, how can you work in filth like this?"' The writers always told them it wasn't that bad, even though it was an unattractive room, devoid of pictures and furniture except for a desk, chairs and filing cabinets. This spartan style was adopted partly on purpose, as Bob explains. 'We weren't there to do anything except sit at a desk and write, and all you need for that is a pad and pencil and two chairs.'

Later, when Bob and his wife moved to their house in Surrey, another office was required, and this time the writers' hunt took them to a room above a greengrocer's shop and petrol station in Billinghurst. The location may have been different, but working together was just as much fun. 'We used to laugh an awful lot, about the stuff we were doing and stuff we couldn't do,' Bob remembers. 'I think most writers, from time to time, go off on little fantasies of their own, inventing scenes that you could never put on television, but it keeps you going on a crazy streak for a couple of hours. You just have fun before saying, "Oh well, now let's get down to work." They were great times.'

Esmonde and Larbey's first hit came in 1968, with *Please, Sir!* The antics of Class 5C and their callow teacher, Bernard Hedges (played by John Alderton), who had the unenviable task of trying to teach Fenn Street Secondary Modern's most infamous bunch, made good viewing and LWT's sitcom quickly became a success. Over a four-year period, 57 episodes were recorded.

As Bob Larbey explains, it was Frank Muir who afforded them the opportunity. 'Frank was Head of Entertainment at LWT and he pulled in all the writers he'd worked with or knew, and we were two of them. He asked whether we had any ideas, and we replied, "We've got this wonderful idea – it's about a faded concert pianist who's now doing end-of-the-pier work. He's living in boarding houses but refuses to change his lifestyle. He's lavish with tips and sends flowers to all the girls at the end of the show. What

do you think about that, Frank?" He replied, "I hate that. Have you got any other ideas?" So we told him about a half-idea we'd come up with, about a young teacher at a secondary modern school, and he was interested in that straight away.'

After discussing the idea a little further, Frank Muir commissioned a pilot, and soon after delivering the script Bob and John received a call asking them for a series. Muir was also responsible for recruiting John Alderton. 'He'd seen him doing bits and pieces and thought he would be ideal as the teacher, and of course he was,' says Bob.

'Yes, he was wonderful,' agrees John Esmonde. 'We chose a rough school in a rough area, where a truly dedicated, innocent young teacher had to teach a class who knew more about the world than he did. It's a show I'm proud of.'

Although they can't recall what originally sparked the idea to write a sitcom based in a school, Bob Larbey believes it was a natural subject to explore. 'Being a bit young at heart, or childish, we still had a fair recall of school, the ambience and all the sounds in the corridors. The tension occurs when you stick this young idealist teacher in the position of having to teach kids who are much more worldly-wise than himself.

'We had a very good cast, with Deryck Guyler back again as the caretaker, Joan Sanderson, and, of course, John Alderton, which was a bonus in itself because it gave us the opportunity to bring a comparatively new face, certainly in situation comedy, into the lead role – and the nation took to him instantly.'

The speed with which *Please, Sir!* became a hit with viewers surprised the writers. 'It was hugely popular. We've always considered our shows to be slow-burners, but that one clicked almost immediately.' Such success engendered a sense of confidence in their ability as professional writers. 'We were being asked to do more and more, and it was then that we started thinking, "We've actually made it. We really don't have to go back to work!"'

Many of the characters that Esmonde and Larbey created in *Please, Sir!* were so popular that a sequel was written, exploring the kids' lives post-Fenn Street Secondary. Although *The Fenn Street Gang* never hit

the heights of *Please, Sir!*, 49 episodes were made. 'It didn't last so long because John Alderton wanted to move on, which is perfectly right and proper, but LWT were unwilling to let this thing go, it had become so popular,' says Bob. 'They reckoned we could retain some interest, even without John Alderton, just by following the kids along. It worked to some extent, but was never as good as the original.'

The Fenn Street Gang led to another spin-off. In the second series George Baker played a character named Bowler, and he was so successful that LWT commissioned thirteen episodes that studied the character's early life.

The 1970s was a busy decade for Esmonde and Larbey, and by 1975 they had two shows running in tandem. While *The Good Life* was entertaining viewers on BBC1, LWT were screening the first of 34 episodes of *Get Some In!*, a sitcom about national service. When the writers were looking around for a new idea for LWT, they had called upon their personal experience again. 'We asked ourselves whether

Left to right: **Derrick Goodwin, John Esmonde, Bob Larbey and Humphrey Barclay meet in London to discuss new ideas.**

there was anything else we knew about, and suddenly thought of national service. We'd both done two years of it, so it seemed an obvious choice,' says Bob. But their idea for a service-based show was initially rejected. 'We took it to London Weekend, who didn't like it, so we ran down to Thames and sold it to Philip Jones, who loved it.'

Bob believes that one of the reasons the show was popular was that a lot of people could still remember their days in the forces. 'Many people still had fond, or otherwise, memories of national service, and for those who were too young it was still interesting, because they'd heard about it but never experienced it. They couldn't believe that corporals, like the one played by Tony Selby, could be so beastly.'

'The ogre of a corporal was common,' smiles John. 'National service was a time in a man's life when he came up against someone with absolute power, but couldn't do anything about it because he was captive and of a lesser rank. It's funny now, but was quite painful at the time.'

Esmonde and Larbey's busy schedule continued when they contemplated their next project, another sitcom for the Beeb. The final series of *The Good Life* had already been transmitted and *Get Some In!* was nearing completion when, in November 1977, Richard Briers first appeared as habitual liar Ralph Tanner, alongside Michael Gambon as Brian Bryant. Two series of *The Other One* were made, but the sitcom wasn't well received by either viewers or critics, even though the writers count it among their own favourite pieces of work. 'I've got a very soft spot for it,' admits John. Perhaps part of the reason for the show's lack of success was the public's reluctance at the time to accept Richard Briers, who had a proven track record of playing the benevolent good guy, as an unscrupulous character. This is something that disappoints John Esmonde: 'I thought he was brilliant, but the audiences didn't like seeing their nice Richard as a rotter.'

The mood of the people is extremely capricious, making it virtually impossible for programme-makers and writers to hit the right note every time. Although Esmonde and Larbey are one of the nation's most successful writing partnerships, with many classic shows to their credit, they've tasted failure, too. Not only was *The Other One* not readily accepted by viewers, but their football sitcom *Feet First* and *Just Liz* starring Sandra Payne and Rodney Bewes (both for Thames) as well as *Down to Earth* (for the BBC) all finished after just one series. 'It's difficult putting your finger on why something doesn't work,' says Bob Larbey with a wry smile. 'It's very easy to lash out and blame all manner of things, but usually it's a mix of reasons. Word of mouth is always very interesting – when you have a hit show on your hands, friends and neighbours come out with things like "Oh it's so funny, I loved the last episode," but for shows that are not doing so well they just say "I saw your show last night" and that's it. When you get that response, you *know* things are not working.'

Their 1995 sitcom *Down to Earth* featured Richard Briers as Tony Fairfax, who returns to England after

nearly four years of working as cultural adviser in a South American 'banana republic'. The first episode was transmitted on 5 January of that year, and when Bob and his wife had finished watching the programme, they knew it was in trouble. 'As far as the writing process was concerned, John and I had collaborated in the normal way and enjoyed doing it, as well as reading the script to each other. John was holidaying in Spain so he missed the screening, but as soon as it ended I realized that neither my wife nor I had laughed. I don't normally sit and shriek with laughter at my own work, but I do react with the occasional chuckle, while my wife will usually have a really good laugh. But this time we just looked at each other, and all I could utter was "Ummm!". That just about sums it up. I couldn't say where we got it wrong, but it just didn't work and wasn't our best writing.

'Somehow Richard's character didn't appeal. A lot of people objected to him not playing his usual role of Mr Nice Guy. In *The Other One* we had a great pairing with Richard Briers and Michael Gambon. That was my favourite, and we all had a great time. But all the same, it never lit up. One reason, in my opinion, was that for once Richard wasn't cast as a sympathetic character. He was the shark, the loud-talking braggart. Back then, when audiences saw Richard performing that kind of part they often recoiled and thought, "Oh no, that's not our Richard."'

More recent guest appearances in dramas such as *Inspector Morse* and *Midsomer Murders*, as well as excursions into Shakespeare with Kenneth Branagh, have highlighted Richard Briers' versatility, and his many admirers are now more relaxed about seeing him turn his hand to roles other than comedy nice-guys, which has enabled him to overcome one of the greatest challenges facing any successful comedy actor.

Despite this setback, thanks to adept writing and casting John Esmonde and Bob Larbey went on to score another huge hit starring Richard Briers. The first of 27 episodes of *Ever Decreasing Circles* graced our screens in 1984, with Richard playing the insufferable organizer Martin Bryce, whose obsession with minutiae almost drove his friends and his wife, played by Penelope Wilton, insane. This was sitcom-writing at its best, and as far as Bob is concerned a large part of the show's popularity is down to the 'little bit of Martin in all of us'.

John agrees: 'A lot of the success in television writing – or any writing, for that matter – is about recognizing something, leaving the viewers thinking "I know someone like that" or "That's Dad all over again". And that's what we got with Martin in *Ever Decreasing Circles*.'

The writers also relished the chance to work with Briers again. 'Richard is such a bloody good actor, he really is – and he's a nice bloke, too. We've always got on well, and John and I were able to write speeches that flowed very easily from his mouth. In *Ever Decreasing Circles*, for example, his wife's name is Ann, and he always had a sort of twang in his voice whenever he said it. It was like "Aenne", and that was exactly the way we would have said it, with a slight whine, if somebody had asked us to pronounce her name. Richard always got that sort of thing in one.

'We've always had an affinity with Richard. He said our lines perfectly every time, just the way we'd written them. The inflection, everything, would be immaculate. But you can get other, equally good, actors and actresses who won't be able to pick up on that. They'll put the inflection somewhere else, and although it'll still be funny, they won't say it quite the way you intended. But Richard would. Part of the attraction is that he makes you laugh a lot, and he's one of the best performers at the first read-through that I've ever come across.'

Although John and Bob find it hard to pinpoint the precise moment they conceived the idea for *Ever Decreasing Circles*, the Martin Bryce character was influenced partly by an amateur footballer they knew. 'Bob and I used to play old boys' football, and we had regular meetings to talk about subs, match fixtures, things like that. But this chap would arrive with a briefcase and give a dissertation on how to take a penalty. Now think of that happening in someone's front room, with this chap, who was certainly no lithe athletic type, being unbelievably English in his fairness but at the same time really frustrating. He was always painfully keen. I remember one week we were playing a match and didn't have a referee, so he decided that he'd be the ref and play as

well. As you can imagine, that's quite difficult! He even scored – after which he apologized to everyone on the other side.'

This was just one of the influences behind the series, because, as John Esmonde points out, 'The spark behind any series usually has several prongs. I remember thinking about the mental machinations of the character. Of course Martin was terribly tortured, he had so many little bees and bugs in him.' Martin was heading at full steam towards a nervous breakdown, with his self-inflicted obsessions dragging him down like quicksand. 'If you're that way inclined, all these little worries inhabit the brain, and to write about that, as opposed to the problems of a professional schoolteacher for example, is a different form of writing, though not necessarily more difficult.'

Even though *Ever Decreasing Circles* contained its fair share of laughs, it was also full of realism. 'Martin's hang-ups were amusing, yet totally realistic, because I'm sure there are plenty of people who can't stand telephone wires getting tangled up, road-sweepers leaving cigarette stubs behind, molehills, awkward-looking odd numbers – just some of the aspects of life that irked Martin terribly. I hope it was true to life, coming from the idiosyncracies of a particular mentality. Martin could see the perfect world on the horizon, but he never quite reached it.'

One aspect of Esmonde and Larbey's writing that helped *Ever Decreasing Circles* rise above many of its competitors of the period was the occasional focus on pathos. In one particular episode Martin believes his wife is having an affair with 'Mr Perfect' – alias Paul Ryman, wonderfully played by Peter Egan – while in the final chapter Martin discovered he was to become a father, a prospect that, for a time, worried him. These situations were observed beautifully through the script, something John Esmonde puts down to experience. 'By that time we'd been writing for some years and felt confident enough to explore this sort of topic.'

Another touching scene finds Ann telling Paul Ryman how Martin has helped get her life back on track, and, although he can infuriate her, she stresses how much she loves him. 'By that point,' says Bob, 'a lot of people were saying, "How in God's name does she put up with him? Why doesn't she kill him, or divorce him?" So we thought we had to put a little bit of shoring-up timber in the material to explain why she loved him. After all, he was a good man at heart. John and I used to say that you wouldn't want to spend ten minutes in a pub with Martin, you'd have to get out, but you'd never think of him as nasty. If your house caught fire, he'd be the first to arrive with a bucket of water.'

Bob Larbey has recently been watching repeats of *Ever Decreasing Circles* on satellite, and he admits that they still make him laugh. 'It's another of my favourites. Everybody says they know someone like Martin. We got the idea of someone who wanted life to be perfect, who wanted life to fall into place around him, to the point of being neurotic. Then we asked ourselves, "What would really rock that particular boat?" The answer was a nearby Mr Perfect who breezed through life getting everything right – and it worked.'

One question the writers are always being asked is whether there's any chance of reviving some of their best-loved shows, such as *The Good Life* and *Ever Decreasing Circles*, but it's a suggestion Bob swiftly dismisses. 'I met Harold Snoad, who produced the final two series of *Ever Decreasing Circles*, a couple of years ago, and he was keen to bring it back. He had plenty of ideas, but it's something I can't do, not after such a gap. Unless you do what Dick Clement and Ian La Frenais did with *Whatever Happened to the Likely Lads?*, which was brilliant – even better than *The Likely Lads* itself – and revive the show within a relatively short period, I don't think it would work. You can't leave something for ten, fifteen years and then revisit it.'

The era of Martin Bryce concluded on Christmas Eve 1989, by which stage the writers felt it was time to move on to new projects. 'We were ready to bring it to an end. The show had become very popular after some repeats, and was doing extremely well. But, like everything, it had a limited life,' explains Bob. 'Maybe we were right, maybe we were wrong – I don't know. But we just felt that four series was enough, and this meant we were able to end it once and for all, with Martin leaving The Close for a new life.'

Esmonde and Larbey continued writing throughout the 1980s and early 1990s, most notably with *Brush Strokes*, starring Karl Howman as painter and decorator Jacko, which ran to five series. The last sitcom they penned together was the ill-fated *Down to Earth*, after which they called it day. But their decision to dissolve the partnership was not based on the sitcom's lack of success – they were far too battle-hardened for that. 'We'd actually decided before the show was even commissioned that it would be our last,' explains Bob. 'The whole thing was coming to a natural end. I for one wanted to be at home more, particularly in the winter. Having to travel and sit in a manky office with a two-bar electric fire no longer appealed.'

'John was also leaning more and more towards a life in Spain, so we agreed, when we wrote the first series, that if the BBC liked it and wanted us to go on we'd get together and just write that, for as long as it lasted. But we weren't taking on any more joint commissions.'

Age was another factor that had to be taken into consideration. 'I'm 62 now, and we've been writing for about 33 years, which adds up to a lot of writing,' says John Esmonde. 'I wanted to spend more of my time in Spain, where I now live, so it seemed the right time to call it a day.'

ESMONDE & LARBEY'S TV TRACK RECORD

The Dick Emery Show (first shown 1963) – various sketches for the BBC

Room at the Bottom (1966–67) – 8 episodes for the BBC

Just Good Friends (1967) – a pilot was screened locally by ABC (Midlands and North) as part of the station's 'Comedy Tonight' feature but no series was made

Please, Sir! (1968–72) – 45 (out of 57) episodes for LWT

Who Sleeps on the Right? (1970) – one episode for LWT's 'The Mating Machine' series

The Fenn Street Gang (1971–73) – 37 (out of 49) episodes for LWT

Cosmo and Thingy (1972) – 1 episode for LWT

Bowler (1973) – 13 episodes for LWT

Football Crazy (1974) – 1 episode for Thames

The Good Life (1975–8) – 30 episodes for the BBC

Get Some In! (1975–8) – 34 episodes for Thames

Three Piece Suite (1977) – extended sketch for the BBC

The Other One (1977–9) – 13 episodes for the BBC

Feet First (1979) – 7 episodes for Thames

Just Liz (1980) – 6 episodes for Thames

Don't Rock the Boat (1982–3) – 12 episodes for Thames

Now and Then (1983–4) – 13 episodes for LWT

Ever Decreasing Circles (1984–7, 1989) – 27 episodes for the BBC

Brush Strokes (1986–91) – 40 episodes for the BBC

Double First (1988) – 7 episodes for the BBC

Hope It Rains (1991–2) – 13 episodes for Thames

Mulberry (1992–3) – 13 episodes for the BBC

Down to Earth (1995) – 7 episodes for the BBC

BOB LARBEY'S SOLO TV CREDITS INCLUDE:

A Fine Romance (1981-84) – 26 episodes for LWT

The Curious Case of Santa Claus (1982) – comedy film for C4

On the Up (1990-92) – 19 episodes for BBC

The Darling Buds of May (1991–3) – 4 (out of 20) episodes for Yorkshire

As Time Goes By (1992–) – 47 episodes for BBC

My Good Friend (1995–6) – 14 episodes for Anglia

ESMONDE & LARBEY'S RADIO OUTPUT FOR EDWARD TAYLOR

Three on the Town was broadcast as part of *Star Parade* on Sunday, 1 September 1963 at 2.30pm. As well as Eric Barker, Kenneth Connor and Wallace Eaton, the half-hour programme featured Percy Edwards, Roy Dotrice, Norma Ronald, Gordon Faith and the Gordon Franks Quartet. Edward Taylor produced the programme, and it was repeated on Thursday, 5 September at 8pm.

Two series of *You're Only Old Once* were transmitted. The first series started on Sunday, 11 February 1968 and went out on Radio 1 and 2 at 9.30pm. Produced by Edward Taylor, the first instalment – 'The Pride of the Regiment' – boasted a cast of Clive Dunn, Deryck Guyler, Joan Sanderson, Patricia Hayes, Harry Webster, Carleton Hobbs and Gordon Clyde. The show was pre-recorded at The Playhouse, Northumberland Avenue, London WC2.

The second series kicked off with the episode 'Combined Operations' and went out on Radio 2 at 2.31pm on Sunday, 1 June 1969. As well as the three main cast members, Patricia Hayes, Harry Webster and Hilda Braid also featured.

You're Only Old Once

Episode	Transmission date
SERIES ONE:	
The Pride of the Regiment	11 February 1968
Home from Home	18 February 1968
The Old Flame	25 February 1968
Too Many Cooks	3 March 1968
Matron's Choice	10 March 1968
Go to War on an Egg	17 March 1968
A Visitor for Today	24 March 1968
Man of Letters	31 March 1968
SERIES TWO:	
Combined Operations	1 June 1969
Just the Job	8 June 1969
The Joys of Motoring	15 June 1969
Room for One More	22 June 1969
The Great Escape	29 June 1969
Two Tickets to Paris	6 July 1969
Mr Lewis Rides Again	13 July 1969
The Skeleton in the Cupboard	20 July 1969

LENDING A HELPING HAND

Back in the early 1960s, while Esmonde and Larbey's writing partnership was still at an embryonic stage, script editor EDWARD TAYLOR spotted potential in their work and spent time nurturing their talents. The advice, guidance and opportunities he gave the two writers paid dividends when they launched full-time careers and became one of the most successful writing partnerships within the genre of British sitcom. Here, Edward recalls those early days:

In 1963 I'd just taken on the post of Script Editor, BBC Radio Light Entertainment, which involved dealing with all the speculative scripts sent in. They amounted to quite a few in those days. I was also specifically charged with finding new writers and helping launch their careers, and I clearly remember the first script that came from Esmonde and Larbey, via Barry Took.

Barry has always been very supportive of new writers, and although I can't recall why he passed the script to me at the time, I know he felt it had potential and deserved further consideration. It was a revue-style script with the incredible star casting of Hermione Gingold and Anthony Newley – not the right pairing by any means. A lot of it wasn't up to

much, but there were two or three sections that actually made me laugh.

Most of the material I had to read was gruesomely unfunny, so whenever I found something that made me laugh I had to do something about it. I invited John and Bob in to see me, but as they already had full-time jobs and couldn't make it during the day, we agreed to meet in the evenings at the BBC. After a full day's work, you'd think they'd have been tired when we met. But no, they were always eager, and would happily have come in more often if I'd let them.

I was able to use some of their work on one or two sketch shows we were doing at the time. I'd just started *I'm Sorry, I'll Read That Again* and I think we used some of their stuff in that. But I told them the way forward was to write a situation comedy, and we sat down and discussed the idea. Another series I'd been involved in launching was *Star Parade*, which aimed to promote new writers, just like *Comedy Playhouse* on television. Each show was half an hour long, and I suggested we thought of something for that. Talking amongst ourselves, we came up with an idea of a farmer stranded in London with a pig because he's arrived too late for an agricultural show. The cast consisted of Eric Barker, a great comedian of years gone by, Wallace Eaton, from radio's *Take It From Here*, and Kenneth Connor, playing a policeman who kept turning up every five minutes.

The programme, called *Three on the Town*, went out as part of *Star Parade* and was quite well received. When the controllers of the Light Programme held an inquest on all the *Star Parade* offerings, no one felt that *Three on the Town* would run for any length of time, so it never became a series. However, I said we had a funny policeman in the show and suggested giving him a series of his own. The idea took off and Kenneth Connor was cast in *Spare a Copper*, which became Esmonde and Larbey's first situation comedy. It didn't let anybody down and did quite nicely, although we only did two series.

By this time I was meeting John and Bob about once a week, always in the evening, to discuss ideas. I can't remember who, but one of us came up with the idea for a comedy in an old folks' home, which at that stage hadn't been done before. We developed the idea and came up with *You're Only Old Once*, with Clive Dunn and Deryck Guyler, two actors who specialized in playing old dodderers. Hattie Jacques was going to play the matron but had to pull out, so I got Joan Sanderson instead. We did two series of that, and it was going along very nicely. I think it could have run longer, but by then Bob and John, understandably, wanted to go for the big money by writing for television. I had them exclusively for radio for about three years, and it was an enjoyable period.

They managed to get their foot in the door on television with *Room at the Bottom*, which didn't take off, but then they sold *Please, Sir!* – at which point, I'm afraid, they skipped out of my life. But I enjoyed working with them.

Right from day one John and Bob had the ability to come up with funny lines, funny ideas and funny situations, which is priceless. You can have would-be writers who send you a neat, literate, intelligent script, but it doesn't actually make you laugh. Then someone else sends in a scruffy script, with lots of rubbish in it, but if you go through it you discover that on page six there's something that makes you roar with laughter. Once you've found that, you have to persevere, getting rid of the dross and mining the gold. Then, of course, the writers need the stamina and determination to go along with you, and John and Bob had that. They not only had the ability to write material that was funny, but also the grit to keep at it.

I expected them to do well on television, but I certainly didn't predict they'd do as well as they did. I was also surprised when they moved into a fairly sophisticated area of comedy writing. I always regard *The Good Life*, *Ever Decreasing Circles* and some of their other shows as sophisticated. During the time I was working with them, their ideas were fairly broad and slightly down-market – a direction I encouraged, because there's nothing wrong with writing in such a style. I thought that was their forte, and was agreeably surprised when they started writing some serious comedy.

The Good Life had a novel storyline and was a very good idea. Obviously the show was helped along by the cast. I enjoyed the programme, and although I wasn't an avid follower I watched it whenever I could. It was a very civilized, amusing and sympathetic piece of writing. Richard Briers, as a light comedian, I could watch all week. Felicity Kendal is, of course, totally delicious and I could watch her most of the week, too, but Penelope Keith and Paul Eddington were equally good – it was very well cast.

RICHARD BRIERS

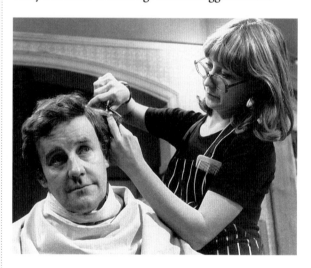

TOM GOOD

On reaching one of life's most frightening junctures, Tom Good is brave (some might say foolhardy) enough not only to take stock of his life but to do something radical about it. They say life begins at forty, and for Tom it certainly does.

It's eight years since he joined JJM Ltd as a draughtsman on the same day as his friend Jerry Leadbetter. But while Jerry's career is flourishing, Tom's lack of ambition and ever-increasing urge to break free from nine-to-five drudgery have relegated him to a stagnant backwater in middle management. Tired of constant commuting, earning a meagre salary and reluctant to live out his days making plastic animals to go into cereal packets, on the threshold of middle age Tom decides to jack it all in and attempt a life of self-sufficiency – in, of all places, smart suburban Surbiton.

Although his loyal wife Barbara supports his decision to give up a secure job and risk all, Tom rarely considers her feelings in his struggle to make

a success of his new lifestyle. If courage, joviality and determination are some of his strengths, obstinacy and chauvinism are undoubtedly among his weaknesses.

Tom sees life as an adventure, and his habit even now of reading the *Boys' Book of Knowledge*, coupled with his proud ownership of a collection of toy soldiers, indicates that there remains a substantial part of him that has never grown up.

When the offer to play Tom Good came along, Richard Briers considered his options very carefully before accepting the role. 'Apart from the money, I wasn't sure if a return to situation comedy was right for me. I had to ask myself whether I wanted to be a TV personality or a more serious sort of actor, performing at the Old Vic

But my part was all about a guy in a dull office who became a fanatic at something, and I had to spend time building the character.'

At the beginning, Richard feared that the show's stockbroker-belt setting would limit its appeal. 'Initially I thought of it as a very pleasant middle-class show, but perhaps a little narrow. I saw it appealing

and places like that. In hindsight, it was silly thinking, but I was young and perhaps a little pretentious. I'm delighted now that I made the decision to play Tom, because I owe a lot to the exposure I received in *The Good Life*.'

Since Tom Good had no really extreme personality traits or foibles to exploit, Richard decided to model the character on himself. 'There wasn't a great deal in the man to latch on to, whereas someone like Margo was a strongly written character – a wonderful one!

mostly to people in the south of England. But of course, the moment Tom Good left his job, picked up his spade and dug into the earth, it became classless. From then on, people from all walks of life began to enjoy it, because everyone knows about trying to fend for yourself or do your own thing. Most people, at some time in their lives, have thought they'd like to be their own boss, so it hit a nerve with the wider public.'

Richard enjoyed playing Tom Good, egotistical as the character was. 'He was a very selfish man. They had no children and his wife had no decent clothes – her sacrifice was wonderful. They obviously adored each other, otherwise she wouldn't have gone along with Tom's plans, but he was still an old bugger!'

The first two series by no means set the world alight in terms of audience figures, and it was not until the third that the sitcom began to pull in a sizeable audience. Richard feels this is understandable. 'I think it was a matter of getting used to us. When that finally happened, I remember John Howard Davies remarking, "They love you now," and me replying, "Oh, dear, what a responsibility." Being liked is fine, you're paid for that, but when people have a great affection for you, it feels completely different, because you daren't let the standard drop. It's quite a pressure.'

The stress of maintaining the standard was eased by the high morale that built up within the tightly-knit team. Such was the team spirit among the actors, production team and writers that everyone felt free to air their views regarding any aspect of the show – one example of this being the time Richard suggested introducing the occasional altercation between the Goods. 'I felt Barbara and Tom were getting too lovey-dovey and that we needed to have the odd row, just to keep it real. After all, poor Barbara was putting up with so much. John and Bob agreed to write some scenes along those lines, and we ended up having a couple of real flare-ups, which was great.'

Richard particularly remembers a scene in the 1978 episode 'The Last Posh Frock', in which the glamorous Eileen, Barbara's old schoolfriend, comes to dinner and Barbara has only a worn-out skirt and top to wear. 'Tom was giving Eileen the eye and Barbara was livid,' he recalls. 'She ended up pouring gravy down the front of her blouse and declaring, "I'm not a woman, I'm a Barbara." That was splendid, because the writers had brought a little sexism into the script.'

Like the rest of the cast, Richard enjoyed making the four series, but when Esmonde and Larbey decided to bring their self-sufficiency sitcom to an end, he respected their decision. 'They realized they weren't going to be able to go on producing fresh storylines for the scripts, so – unlike shows today, where themes seem to be repeated – they took it off when we were right at the top.

'On any show, the most important person is the scriptwriter. But, as the writer, if you get to the point of thinking, "Oh, no, I've got to come up with yet another script", it's not going to be any good. You need the kind of inspiration that makes you say, "God, I've got a great idea for episode seven!" Once that stops, you're really in it just for the money and the heart will go out of it. We were so lucky to have two terrific writers who had high standards.'

Since Tom Good had no extreme personality traits, Richard Briers decided to model the character on himself.

Reflecting on his busy television career, Richard regards *The Good Life* as his favourite sitcom. 'I owe so much to it, and it was the show that gave people the most amusement. I enjoyed *Ever Decreasing Circles* and *The Other One*, too, but this was the big success, which made big stars out of us all. Paul Eddington, for example, was a first-class actor, but before *The Good Life* he was always playing supporting roles. Jerry made him, and when he went on to get *Yes, Minister* he made serious money for the first time in his life.'

Shortage of money is something Richard has experienced at first hand. Financial security has always been a driving force in his life, partly because it's something his parents never had. 'My father was a

rolling stone, always moving from job to job, and money was extremely short. He lived for the day, never thinking about tomorrow, and growing up in that environment made me the opposite – I'm very cautious,' he admits. When his career began to take off, Richard started saving as much as possible, knowing only too well that the acting world is a precarious one. 'Now I'm back to being a jobbing actor, playing character parts, but it doesn't matter too much, because while I was a leading actor in TV I made sure I used my money wisely, clearing the mortgage and getting all my other commitments sorted out.'

While Richard's father drifted between jobs, his mother dreamt of pursuing a showbiz career herself.

'She was frustrated because she was a good pianist and might have made it professionally,' he says. 'But I came along and that put a stop to her dream, because there wouldn't have been enough money to hire a nanny to take care of me.'

Born in London's Raynes Park in 1934, Richard – who has a younger sister, Jane, an actress and drama teacher – spent his early years in a first-floor flat. 'At the end of the Second World War we moved to Guildford, but later we returned to Raynes Park and the same flat.' His earliest memories are of the Blitz. 'Our area wasn't bombed as badly as the East End, but we got a lot of near misses. I remember collecting shrapnel, and seeing shop windows bulge and explode opposite our flat. So we were quite close to it

all, and a lot of my early memories are coloured by the war.'

Richard couldn't wait to leave school, a period of his life that holds few fond memories, to put it mildly. 'I hated it!' he declares. 'Apart from the fact that I ran the school's discussion group, I was hopeless, partly because I never listened. I was useless at maths, but I liked English and was able to write a good essay.'

After leaving school at sixteen with no formal qualifications, Richard took a clerical post with a London cable manufacturer, even though he already had ambitions to become an actor. 'I was about eight when I started reading aloud in the kitchen – because it had an echo, which made me sound rather good – so the ego was already in place,' he remembers with a smile. 'I started amateur acting at fourteen but had no idea how to make a career of it.'

Thanks to his father, who knew the boss, Richard secured a job as a junior clerk, which meant undertaking menial jobs in a department issuing share certificates. Although his duties were far from stimulating, he was only too pleased to be contributing to the family's small income. 'My main responsibility was getting in on time to make the tea,' he says. 'I was also in charge of keeping the office's filing system tidy and franking all the letters, which I'd post on my way home. I was very keen at first and even thought about becoming a salesman, but I soon discovered I'd have to be qualified in electrical engineering. As I'm hopeless with technology, I didn't hold out much hope.' Richard even went to evening classes for a while in an attempt to qualify, but claims he couldn't understand a word that was being said. This could, of course, be put down to the fact that, by mistake, he attended the second-year class instead of the first!

Quickly coming to the conclusion that he had no real interest in the subject, Richard knuckled down to his job as filing-clerk-cum-tea-boy, which earnt him two pounds ten shillings a week. He was comforted by the thought that once the tedious working day was over he'd be off doing the one thing he truly loved, acting, in an amateur group. 'I knew in the back of my mind that I wanted to be a full-time actor, but didn't know how to go about it.'

A turning point came when his boss asked him to sign an application form for the company pension scheme. To the eighteen-year-old Richard this form seemed to symbolize the beginning of the end of his life. 'I was so terrified, I couldn't bring myself to sign it. I realized that, unless I did something quickly, I'd be working there for the rest of my life.' His predicament was resolved by the receipt of his national service call-up papers, which provided him with a legitimate reason for leaving the firm. However, he soon found himself working as a filing clerk again in the RAF. He was based for two years at Northwood, where location work for *The Good Life* was later filmed.

His first taste of amateur acting had been at Wimbledon at the age of fourteen, before joining the Regent Street Polytechnic two years later. During his national service he joined the Elephant and Castle Poly, thanks to actor Brian Murphy, whom he met in the RAF. 'We used to traipse over there two or three times a week – it was great fun,' he recalls.

Richard's experiences as an amateur actor stood him in good stead when he joined RADA after leaving the RAF, but he also had to face the ignominy of being thrown out of one production. While performing with the Regent Street Poly, he was asked to leave because he spoke so fast that no one could understand him. 'I was heartbroken at being sacked. It hurt a lot. I started taking lessons, to try and slow my speech down. It was sheer nerves, really. Luckily, RADA sorted me out, even though I've always had a tendency to rush my lines, and do even now.'

Years later, well after he had made good as an actor, Richard bumped into the director who had given him the push so long ago. 'He said, "I feel so embarrassed about it," but I told him not to be because I'd needed training. After all, it's useless if you can't hear what someone's talking about. You've *got* to sack them!' Through experience and training, Richard learnt how to control his rapid delivery of lines and even exploit it for his own benefit.

He spent two invaluable years at RADA, where his contemporaries included the likes of Albert Finney and Peter O'Toole. 'Some people are naturals, but I wasn't. I was very stiff and tense, and couldn't move well on stage, so I had to be painstakingly taught. Every term I got a little better, though, and finally I ended up winning a scholarship to Liverpool Repertory Company, which was wonderful.' The scholarship entailed working in three-weekly rep for fifteen months – a superb apprenticeship for any young actor.

His stint at Liverpool was also rewarding for another important reason. It was there that he met his future wife. Soon after meeting actress Ann Davies, who was acting as stage manager there at the time, Richard borrowed five quid off her mum to

THE SAME OLD TUNE...

Throughout the sitcom Tom Good is often heard whistling the same old tune. Richard Briers explains, 'It's the opening bars of *Over the Rainbow*, which just happens to be a favourite of mine. It's not something I was asked to do by the producer or the writers, I just introduced it off my own bat.'

buy an engagement ring, and within six months they were married.

After Liverpool, Richard and Ann spent six months at the Belgrave Theatre, Coventry, before moving to London and playing Outer London reps. Richard's West End debut quickly followed. 'The play starred John Clements and Kay Hammond, who were marvellous. John was so helpful, he was like a father-figure to me, allowing me the focus on stage, which was very unselfish of him. I really enjoyed the part, it was very funny.'

Richard rates those early repertory years as some of the best of his career. 'We were young, employed and playing some big parts, in some lovely old theatres, too, whereas most kids today have to make do with pub theatre. I was making £8 a week at Liverpool, while Ann was earning £10 because she was stage manager as well. We didn't have any kids or any responsibilities, and didn't worry about saving – we were very happy-go-lucky, just like my father. In those days I was so enthusiastic that I would happily have slept in the theatre, I loved it so much, whereas, as you get older, you can't wait to get home.'

As Richard's career blossomed it took time for his parents to share their son's optimism about his chosen lifestyle. 'They were very sceptical, because they didn't visit the theatre much. They'd go and see the Crazy Gang at Victoria Palace perhaps once or twice a year, but that was about it. I don't think they could work out how I'd make it in the profession. They thought the acting world was full of glamorous, beautiful people with big personalities. Looking like I did, and do now, I was hardly going to be a sex symbol in the movies! Father was worried and wanted me to work in a bank, while my mother, deep down, quite liked the idea, because she'd always been artistic herself.'

While making his West End debut, Richard was spotted by writers Denis Norden and Frank Muir, who were adapting Henry Cecil's 1955 book *Brothers in Law*, already a successful film starring Ian Carmichael, for the small screen. So impressed were they by Briers' performance that they cast him in the leading role as the credulous legal rookie, Roger Thursby.

At the age of twenty-seven, it was Richard's first starring role. 'It was a challenge, but I was always good at playing emotional, highly-strung people. I've played a lot of them during my career, right up to and including Martin in *Ever Decreasing Circles*, so it was natural for me. But my performance was nearly scuppered by the director, who wasn't very good at getting close-ups. My main talent in comedy is facial reactions!'

Appearing alongside him in *Brothers in Law* was actor/writer Richard Waring, who, a year later, scripted a new sitcom he had devised, in which Briers was given the male lead opposite Prunella Scales.

Waring had always pictured Richard as newly-wed George Starling in *Marriage Lines*, which ran to five series. 'The public liked the show, and it put me right on the map,' says Briers.

Some actors find the transition from stage to screen a little daunting, but Richard, whose television career was progressing nicely, feels the training he had received in rep helped enormously. 'It was the greatest training of all. You learnt how to act sincerely and truthfully. Rep training is the best, and later in life, if you get a part that's particularly difficult, you can fall back on a strong technique, all learnt from those happy days.'

Although Richard has appeared in many hit TV shows, albeit mainly sitcoms, he'll always be best remembered as Tom in *The Good Life*, a part he's proud of. 'It was a rewarding show,' he says. 'The laughter and affection we got from the public was wonderful, and we were well paid for it, too. You can't look down on something that creates that sort of reaction, it did nothing but good for us all. I remember saying to Penelope Keith, "When our obituaries come out, it won't be Shakespeare I'll be remembered for, it'll be *The Good Life* – and you'll be remembered for Margo, whatever other work you do."'

Since *The Good Life* had been written specifically as a vehicle for Richard, at an early stage he met up with the writers, John Esmonde and Bob Larbey (the start of a lucrative relationship), to discuss the project and share his thoughts on casting. 'I've always taken sitcom seriously and, it may sound pompous, but you really do need to have good actors. If you don't find the right blend it shows, and that can spoil the product. Luckily, everyone involved in *The Good Life* got on

really well. We'd all come from the same background, having done years of theatre work, and we quickly built up a friendship. And that warmth came across in the show, I think. It was a cast from heaven. I became very close to Paul Eddington, as he and I were ideally suited in temperament. His character was sophisticated and quiet, while I was clownish and highly energized – we just seemed to match extremely well.'

Think of Richard Briers and a myriad of hit shows spring to mind, but even he has experienced his fair share of failure. One example is *The Other One*, also written by Esmonde and Larbey, which didn't achieve the ratings he had expected. In it Richard was cast as Ralph Tanner, a compulsive liar, and Michael Gambon as Brian Bryant. When the first series of *The Other One* was transmitted in 1977 it didn't take off, even though it was Bob Larbey's favourite among his sitcoms, and Richard loved it, too. The crux of the problem, as far as the public were concerned, was that it was rather bleak for the comedy genre. 'It was produced by John Howard Davies, but because we all liked it so much, and John had more power than producers today, he said we'd do seven more, and we did. It may not have turned out a hit, but we all loved that series.'

The next big hit on Briers' extensive list of credits did not arrive until 1984, when Bob and John created Martin Bryce. 'They decided to write a sitcom about someone who's a complete prat, and Bob said to me, "Out of all the actors I know, you're the only one who can make Martin sympathetic, because we've written an awful little man!" It was a great part, and the scripts contained a lot of pathos as well as comedy, which I love playing.'

Although *The Good Life* is Richard's favourite series, playing the exasperating Martin in 27 episodes of *Ever Decreasing Circles* was his favourite role. 'Martin is an excellent character part. He got in such a state over everything. He was constantly under self-inflicted stress, and obsessed with minutiae.'

Richard has been a regular on the small screen for more than 25 years, but he's not one for watching himself on TV. 'If I see something like *The Good Life*, it makes me a little sad, because you're watching yourself two decades ago. Now white-haired, I think,

"Where did the last twenty years go?" It's getting a bit alarming,' he grimaces, not entirely in jest. 'But I do enjoy watching other people sit there and laugh at the show.'

Nowadays Richard's appearances on television are primarily character parts, including roles in *Inspector Morse* and *Midsomer Murders*, in which he played a psychopathic vicar. He considers that the genre of sitcom has not fared well in recent years. 'There don't seem to be that many writers any more,' he says. 'The whole climate has changed now, and it's a more hard-hitting style.

'Charm seems to have gone out the window, and actors are very laid back. They don't try to make an impression on people or show off so much. They don't ingratiate themselves like we did. We were always taught that at interviews you must dress smartly, speak well, be pleasant and try to be amusing. Now people can just say, "This is me, take it or leave it." It's a very different attitude, which reflects, I think, on a lot of the sitcoms.'

Richard's career has been dominated by TV and theatre, the latter still being his favourite medium. 'I

don't enjoy long runs any more, but the stage is certainly what I like most.' His least favourite medium is film, because there's no live audience, and he feels his film credits are nothing to write home about. 'I didn't make many films, and most of those I did were pretty bad.'

Then, ten years ago, he met Kenneth Branagh, who has since had a big influence on Richard's career, providing opportunities for him to try his hand, once again, at Shakespeare, both on stage and screen. His credits include *Henry V*, Leonato in *Much Ado About Nothing*, Malvolio in *Twelfth Night* and recently Polonius in Branagh's *Hamlet*.

Richard is very grateful for this break. 'Ken has changed my whole career, and it's an honour to have worked on his productions. It was really through my daughter Lucy that I got to know him. She was a great fan of his when he was younger, and went to see a one-man show he did about Lord Byron at a pub venue. Only about eight people turned up to see him, so afterwards he invited them all for a drink – which is typical Ken. Lucy got chatting with him and thought he was marvellous.

'Later, we went up to Stratford to see him in *Henry V*, and afterwards I asked Lucy whether she wanted to meet him again. She said she was too nervous, but I said he was bound to know who I was because he must have grown up with *The Good Life*, so I persuaded her to come along. We had a chat and got on very well, and Ken seemed to take a liking to me. When I next saw him, at the Lyric, Hammersmith, he asked me, out of the blue, whether I'd like to play Malvolio in *Twelfth Night*. I agreed like a shot, and that's how our relationship started. Next, he directed me as King Lear. We toured it all over the world and it was one of the greatest challenges of my career.'

LARBEY ON BRIERS

The character of Tom Good had to be the linchpin of *The Good Life*, and who better to act as that linchpin than Richard Briers, one of this country's finest comedy actors?

Tom had to be liked. He had to get the viewers on his side and keen for him to win his little revolution, and Richard managed this beautifully. From the moment he ploughed up his own front lawn after quitting a job that was stifling him, the viewers were willing him to succeed.

Tom battled against all the odds with a cheerfulness that could actually have grated – a fine line for any actor to tread. But again, Richard trod it perfectly and never fell off the edge!

Richard is the most cheerful of actors to work with and very unselfish about the distribution of lines. If someone else has the funny line, he'll play to that without looking for a little something extra for himself. Not all actors are known to do this!

Physically, the role of Tom was in fact quite demanding. There really was quite a lot of heavy work to do in that garden. A compensation for Richard, however, must have been that he had to kiss Felicity Kendal at regular intervals. Did I say 'quite demanding'?

FELICITY
KENDAL

BARBARA GOOD

Barbara is unstinting in her devotion to her husband. Willingly sacrificing a comfortable lifestyle in which holidays and dining out were the norm, she stands by him and gives him practical support in his fight to become self-sufficient. It's not only Tom who finds his wife's gutsy nature attractive – it's also alluring to Jerry, who, in 'The Windbreak War' (when everyone was tipsy), admits to having a soft spot for Barbara.

From the moment Richard Briers popped his head round the door of Felicity Kendal's dressing room when she was appearing in the West End production of Alan Ayckbourn's sell-out trilogy *The Norman Conquests*, her career was never the same again. Already a success in live theatre, Felicity was struggling to launch a career on the small screen but had missed out on several television parts. She was delighted, then, when Richard informed her that he was making a TV sitcom about self-sufficiency and asked whether she would consider reading for the part of Barbara Good.

When Felicity was eventually cast as his screen wife, Richard Briers was pleased. 'I knew she was a highly talented performer,' he says, 'and I was always subconsciously looking out for TV wives, because I had quite a few! But to get someone like Felicity, who was clearly brilliant, vivacious and attractive, was ideal.'

From the moment they appeared together in 'Plough Your Own Furrow', the first episode of *The Good Life*, the pair showed a discernible understanding and respect for each other. The partnership was swiftly established, boding well for the sitcom's longevity. 'We were quite eccentric as performers, and the Goods were a bit mad, so it all worked fine,' explains Richard. 'We were both a bit potty, shared the same sense of humour and got on really well. Felicity played Barbara with a delightfully dippy, feminine quality, and I was quite good at playing the ordinary "bloke in the street"-type character, so everything just gelled between us.'

Felicity would have accepted the part even if the script had failed to live up to expectations, because she needed the work, but, luckily, that was not the case. She loved Esmonde and Larbey's writing and couldn't wait to get started. Playing Barbara marked a turning point in her life and for the first time she began to enjoy a degree of security, with offers of work pouring in on the back of the sitcom's eventual success. Felicity quickly became a household name and was highly popular with the viewers, especially men. For many, Barbara Good typified their dream wife: attractive, loyal and supportive to the end.

Until *The Good Life*, Felicity's career – like those of the rest of the cast, with the exception of Richard

Briers – had been dominated by the theatre, and she had had little exposure on television. However, it was only a matter of time before she would make her mark on the small screen, thanks to Esmonde and Larbey's classic.

From very early in her life it seemed inevitable that Felicity Kendal would follow in her parents' footsteps and become a professional actress. Born in Solihull in 1947, she spent most of her childhood overseas, as her parents had formed a strong affection for India while

organizing concert parties there for ENSA during the war. They first took their daughter to India when she was just a baby, but when Mahatma Gandhi was assassinated in 1948 the family feared for their safety and returned to the UK. The next five years were spent touring England and Ireland, but Felicity's parents knew where their future lay and by 1953 were back on Indian soil, travelling that vast country with their touring Shakespeare company. Never in any region for longer than three months, Felicity received little formal education. She grabbed what schooling she could, but by the age of twelve was appearing full-time in her parents' theatre productions.

However, she had had her first taste of the stage much earlier, appearing as a changeling in *A Midsummer Night's Dream* at the tender age of nine months and performing her first speaking part at the age of six, when she played Puck in a later production of the same play. Felicity's performances were a success and soon she began working for her parents' company in earnest, playing more roles as well as working backstage and carrying out duties such as prompting – all of this carried out in tandem with her spasmodic schooling at local convents en route.

By the age of ten she was an official employee of the family theatre company, *The Shakespearean*, earning two rupees a week.

In 1965 the Kendal family's adventures in India became the subject of a movie entitled *Shakespeare Wallah*, one of the early productions of Ismail Merchant and James Ivory. Based on Felicity's father's diaries, the drama follows a troupe of English actors until their tour is interrupted by romance, with Felicity earning 40 rupees a week as Lizzie. Little did she know that the film was to provide the vehicle for her returning to England and launching a career as a professional actress.

When *Shakespeare Wallah* was accepted by the Berlin Film Festival and the equivalent event in London, Felicity was invited by Merchant and Ivory to join them at the festivals, all expenses paid. Seeing this offer as a golden opportunity to broaden her horizons and try her luck in Britain, she accepted the invitation with alacrity. At eighteen Felicity was living with her aunt in Warwickshire, but her hopes of finding work were constantly dashed. Every week she sent off letters to prospective employers, to no avail. As she explained later to Glenda Cooper of *The Independent*, 'I found it very hard to get any work at all … I got nowhere because all the doors were tightly shut. An eighteen-year-old claiming that she has nine years' experience in theatre doesn't really ring true, does it?' Felicity was advised to go to drama school, but was determined not to follow the conventional path of fledgling actors – especially since she had already served a ten-year apprenticeship, learning her trade in classics such as the plays of Shakespeare, Shaw and Sheridan. As far as she could see, there was little to be gained from attending drama school.

This period of struggling to find work was a trying time for Felicity. Until she secured an agent, she spent hours in public telephone boxes desperately trying to fix up auditions. But her tenacity paid off when she was finally offered her first role on television, playing a waitress in an episode of ATV's *Love Story*. This was followed soon afterwards by a part as

a motorcyclist in a BBC play, *The Mayfly and the Frog*, starring John Gielgud. Transmitted in December 1966 as part of the *Wednesday Play* series, this production led to welcome offers of work, beginning with spells at the Oxford Playhouse and at the Globe Theatre in Alan Badel's play, *Kean*.

In 1967 Felicity made her West End debut in *Minor Murder*, and from then on she never looked back. Over the three decades of her career she has appeared in over a hundred West End roles, acting in six Tom Stoppard plays and in Sir Peter Hall's production of the Feydeau farce *An Absolute Turkey*, playing Annie in *Ivanov* (for which she won the *Evening Standard* Best Actress Award), and performing in the revival of George Bernard Shaw's *Heartbreak House* at London's Haymarket Theatre, in which she played snooty Ariadne Utterword to rave notices. Her list of theatre credits is a long one, and although nationwide fame eluded Felicity until she appeared in *The Good Life*, the majority of her career has been spent on the stage.

Although her CV contains little in the way of film work (she has appeared in only a handful of movies, including Ken Russell's *Valentino* of 1977), her small-screen credits include a number of well-loved hits. Many people link Felicity with her successes in the genre of situation comedy, but one of her first real television hits was a drama. In 1975 she appeared in ATV's 13-hour series *Edward the Seventh*, playing Princess Victoria, Queen Victoria's eldest daughter. Based on Philip Magnus's book *King Edward VII* and starring Timothy West, Annette Crosbie, Robert Hardy and Sir John Gielgud, the series covered the lifespan of Queen Victoria's successor.

Directing the series was John Gorrie, who enjoyed working with Felicity. 'She played the princess very convincingly, right through until the character was an old lady. I was quite astonished, because Felicity has a wonderful, slightly gamine personality, and I was delighted with how she handled the whole business of growing old. The make-up was very well done, but instead of doing that terrible thing of "old-age" acting, which never really works, she thought herself into the part and it was very effective.'

John was partly responsible for casting Felicity in the role. Having seen some of her work, including *Shakespeare Wallah*, he knew she was right for the part. 'We were pleased to have her in the series,' he says. 'She was enormously sympathetic, which is almost her greatest quality. She's a very endearing actress. People love her, people warm to her – which is why she was so successful in *The Good Life*.'

Four years later John worked with Felicity again, this time casting her as Viola in his production of *Twelfth Night* for the BBC. Since the plot involves the character pretending to be male, John was looking for an actress who could convincingly be disguised as a boy. 'She's slim, small and was lovely in it. Felicity was enchanting, and very good to work with. She has no delusions of grandeur and works well in a team. I thoroughly enjoyed it.'

By the time *Twelfth Night* was transmitted in 1979, Felicity had just played Barbara Good for the last time. Her versatility had already helped her combine a successful stage career with television work, but many actors struggle to be taken seriously when they cross the divide between comedy and the classics. However, brought up on more than her fair share of Shakespeare, Felicity had no problem making the transition. The blinkered attitudes that often prevent things going so smoothly are condemned by director John Gorrie. 'There's a terrible myth – and snobbery – in this country that if you play comedy you can't do serious stuff, and it's nonsense. Felicity is steeped in the classics, and any actor or actress welcomes the opportunity to do all kinds of work. Comedy is the most difficult thing to do anyway.'

In 1992 another drama success saw Felicity Kendal and her good friend Paul Eddington teaming up as screen husband and wife. *The Camomile Lawn* was

Channel 4's five-episode adaptation of Mary Wesley's best-selling book. Directed by Sir Peter Hall, Felicity, in the part of the ruthless Helena Cuthbertson, again received good reviews. However, this cannot be said of her return to sitcom two years later, when she played American Nancy Belasco in *Honey for Tea*, written by Michael Aitkens. This show survived just one series and was panned by the critics.

Apart from this setback, Felicity enjoyed success with virtually all the situation comedies in which she appeared, most notably *The Good Life* and Carla Lane's *Solo* in 1981–2 and *The Mistress* three years later. Two series of *Solo* were made, with Felicity cast as 30-year-old

Gemma Palmer, who faces all the pitfalls of life as a single woman. The programme was warmly received, as was *The Mistress*, which also ran to a second series. This time Felicity played Maxine, the manageress of a florist's, who has an affair with Luke, played by Jack Galloway in the first series and Peter McEnery in the second.

But without doubt it was playing Barbara Good that brought Felicity Kendal's name to the fore, and she still regards *The Good Life* as one of her favourite jobs. Like everyone else, she never anticipated how successful the show would become, particularly in view of its sluggish start in terms of audience figures. Reflecting on why the show was such a hit, Felicity feels one reason is that it hit a chord with viewers. She once told a reporter: '*The Good Life* was a wonderful show. It succeeded because … it was so well timed. A lot of people were fantasizing about kicking convention and doing something like that, and we provided the escape. They were able to live the fantasy by the fireside without the risk and discomfort of actually doing it.'

ESMONDE ON KENDAL

Kendal?! What do you mean, 'Kendal'? She's not a footballer, you know! Mind you, she no doubt could be one if she wanted – a nippy, goal-conscious striker, probably. Yes, that's what Felicity is, when you're lucky enough to have her as one of the stars of your show.

On the subject of Felicity I will not mention the obvious pluses – lovely actress, smashing person, moderately attractive! Instead, I would like to mention two of her less-publicized abilities: her use of 'auto-rehearse track' and what she could make happen when she finished work.

When a show is rehearsed, the floor of the rehearsal room is colour-taped to indicate where things will go later – walls and so on. At that stage objects like sinks are represented only in the most rudimentary of forms. However, when Felicity rehearsed, everything came alive. 'Barbara moves to sink and turns tap on. Pshhh!' Felicity would turn on this imaginary tap and somehow, because she was so motivated, you could just see the water 'pshhhing' out. To watch her do herself and Pinky and Perky, the two invisible pigs, was stunning.

And what could she make happen when we'd finished work? Well, we all used to go round the corner for a curry. It's well documented that, as a mere girl, Felicity toured India, acting in her parents' theatre company. How romantic, and what a wonderful curry education it must have been.

'Felicity! Felicity! Make sure the waiter knows I don't want the okra cut up in my bhindi bhaji, please.' 'Felicity! Felicity! Would you ask if I can have one of those stuffed things?' With a flurry of the correct lingo, Felicity would always make sure we were all happy.

Lovely actress, smashing person, moderately attractive *and* a curry expert – what more do you want?

PAUL EDDINGTON

JERRY LEADBETTER

Jerry is a hard-working commuter, earning a packet to maintain the lifestyle to which his wife, Margo, has become accustomed. Although he, too, enjoys the rewards of his labour, bubbling beneath the surface is a hankering for a less stressful lifestyle. Battling against the traffic to cross London Bridge every day, he almost envies his neighbours the Goods and the bravery, determination and solidarity they show in their drive to buck the system and live off the land. But, unlike Tom, Jerry doesn't have the kind of spouse who would entertain such an idea – Margo is too caught up in social climbing and pretentiousness.

Jerry originally joined JJM as a mere draughtsman, but when the sitcom kicks off he's earning £18K a year and has a company car and an expense account. Thanks to his ambition, drive, money-munching wife, and not least his willingness to fawn whenever the need arises, he climbs steadily up the corporate ladder.

In due course this culminates in his appointment as managing director, but as quickly as Jerry earns money, his wife spends it – something that evidently irks him, since he comments at one point that you'd think he printed the stuff! Although their relationship appears too formal to allow romance and passion, and Jerry sometimes rebels against Margo's fussiness by sitting with his feet on the sofa smoking cigars and listening to Engelbert Humperdinck's 'Release Me', underneath it all they're a devoted couple.

Paul Eddington loved playing Jerry because the character was the antithesis of himself – as his widow, Tricia, confirms. 'He was nothing like him. Whereas Jerry was determined to become a successful company man even if it meant crawling and letting his boss beat him at golf, Paul would never have done that. He'd have seen him in hell first! Paul wasn't a businessman at all and it was interesting watching him play someone intent on climbing the ladder.' And the differences didn't stop there. 'The sort of lifestyle Jerry provided for his demanding wife, and the sort of house and neighbourhood they had to live in, was so different from the way Paul felt – he was playing a person who was as unlike himself as could possibly be.'

Being cast in the role of Jerry had provided Paul Eddington with a mouth-watering opportunity, and he was determined to make it a success. As with every project he undertook, he instilled elements of himself into his creation of the character. 'It was a lovely challenge for him,' smiles Tricia. 'The funny kind of humour that Jerry had was very much my husband. And of course, as the writers got to know the actors they began writing *for* them, anticipating what Dickie Briers or Paul would say, for example, at a given moment. When that started happening, the series began to fly.'

Playing one of the lead roles in *The Good Life* was something of a departure for Paul, who had usually found himself playing rather sinister characters in TV dramas, but it provided the breakthrough he'd been praying for. 'It was the first time the BBC had thought of him as a comedy actor,' explains Tricia. 'As far as television was concerned, he was always playing characters that were unpleasant or quirky, whereas in the theatre he regularly did comedy. He kept on telling people he was a comedy man and that's what he wanted to do on television.'

When the chance to play Jerry came along, Paul didn't think twice before accepting. His adeptness at

playing comedy was a key factor in the sitcom's eventual success, and the role became a stepping stone to the huge worldwide hit *Yes, Minister* and its sequel, *Yes, Prime Minister*. 'Paul and I were always grateful to John Howard Davies for giving him the chance to show he could be a comedy actor on TV as well as the stage,' says Tricia. 'He'd been a guest in several shows, but this was his first big sitcom part.'

Paul was born in London in 1927, but, because his parents split up when he was young, most of his childhood was spent moving around the country while his mother sought employment. Money was tight, and even though Paul was unclear about his future when he left school in 1943 – by which time he was living in a bedsit in Birmingham with his mother and his sister, Shirley – he was determined not to live the life of poverty that his parents had endured. Whatever job he ended up with, it would have to pay well.

Paul harboured dreams of becoming an artist, but rejected the idea because it was financially insecure and instead joined a local department store, where he earned 35 shillings a week as a junior in the display department. He soon decided he hated the job, and when he heard that a girl he had acted with in a school play had joined RADA, he, too, wanted to pursue a career in acting – the one activity he had enjoyed at school.

After working at the store all day, Paul would rush to the Crescent, a theatre in Birmingham, where he spent many an evening hoping someone would notice him and offer him a job. His wish came true when he was given a bit part, as an epicene policeman, in Ivor Novello's *Full House*, to be performed as part of an amateur arts festival. He enjoyed the experience so much that soon he had left his job at the department store and was heading for Colchester, having been accepted into ENSA's drama division as the ASM's assistant at a wage of £5 a week. He joined the touring party at Colchester, which played at military establishments throughout England, Scotland and Wales.

this period that Paul began to regret his lack of formal training. Fearing that it would be an obstacle to furthering his career, he applied to RADA, who offered him a bursary entitling him to free tuition.

Paul's eventual graduation from RADA was followed by a spell at the Bristol Old Vic, while his girlfriend Tricia was appearing at Southport. The couple's respective work commitments restricted their

When the Second World War broke out, Eddington – who had registered as a conscientious objector – continued to perform with ENSA until a tribunal was called. Although the judge ruled that he could continue with ENSA, the organization declined to keep him on, so Paul was forced to look elsewhere for employment.

After the war he joined Birmingham Rep, where he spent his first six months touring schools in two plays – *The Tempest* and *She Stoops to Conquer*. At this time he was the only person in the company with professional experience, the others all being novices or amateurs, but this changed when he joined the main company, appearing in several productions, such as *1066 and All That*, *The Insect Play* and *The Family Reunion*.

A subsequent five-month stint at Worthing Rep was followed by a spell with a fortnightly repertory company based in Sheffield, where he was to meet his future wife, actress Patricia Scott. It was during

courtship to Sundays only, when they would meet halfway, in Manchester. After their wedding in 1952 they rejoined Sheffield Rep before moving on to Ipswich.

After years of working in regional rep, Paul felt it was time to try his luck in the relatively new medium of television, for which the capital was the only place to be. Unable to afford a mortgage, he rented a room in London while Tricia returned to her parents in Devon, taking their son, Toby, with her. Fortunately for their finances, it wasn't long before Paul was offered his first role on the small screen and appeared live on *Yellow Sands*, recorded in Bristol. This soon led to small parts in other programmes, including an episode of *Dixon of Dock Green* and *The Adventures of Robin Hood*, and even his first movie role, albeit a very minor one, as a sailor in a night shoot for the 1956 film *Sailor Beware*.

During Paul's early career as a jobbing actor he was rarely out of work. Nevertheless, money remained short in the Eddington household, which now included a second son, Hugo. But whenever the family neared the poverty line, an offer of work always seemed to come along. For example, a part in the 1959 film *Jet Storm* enabled Paul to pay his income tax bill. However, it was not until more than a decade later, on landing the role of Jerry Leadbetter in *The Good Life* then going on to achieve further success as James Hacker in *Yes, Minister* and *Yes, Prime Minister*, that Paul was to begin making 'real' money.

His television and stage career developed in tandem, and soon he had not only made his West End debut and paid a return visit to the Bristol Old Vic as lead, but had also appeared in the United States in a Broadway production of *A Severed Head*. By the early 1970s there was not a branch of the profession in which Paul had not gained experience. Now with a family of four to support (since his third son, Dominic, and daughter Gemma came along), he struggled on as a jobbing actor accepting any work that came his way, such as parts in *Hine*, a thriller for Thames TV, and in *Special Branch*, in which he played Mr Strand.

The Good Life, which brought the name of Paul Eddington to the fore, was one of the highlights of his career, as Tricia explains. 'Although it wouldn't have been *the* highlight, Paul regarded it as the role that marked the beginning of his television success. By then, of course, he had already been successful in the theatre, but since the main body of people who watch TV don't go to the theatre, they were unaware of the reputation he'd established. So he had to prove himself all over again.' Although he enjoyed working in television, Paul always regarded himself principally as a theatre actor. 'He preferred the stage,' confirms Tricia, 'but was interested in the techniques of all areas of the profession. He was a real worker who wanted to master every angle.'

As soon as Paul read the scripts for *The Good Life*, he knew he would enjoy appearing in the sitcom. He felt the characters' personalities leapt off the page. 'It was a firm foundation from which four people were to gel,' says Tricia. 'Of course, it's the writing that makes a show, and the more experienced an actor becomes, the easier it is to spot a good script. Paul knew he'd found one here.'

Paul had no difficulty in slotting into the role of Jerry Leadbetter. 'He found the character very easy to play,' remarks Tricia, who recalls a particular joke that her husband shared with fellow-actor Richard Briers. 'Paul was a good gardener and loved DIY – he was a very practical man. He used to make a joke of the fact that Dickie, who didn't know one end of a spade from the other, was playing the self-sufficient person, while he was playing the one who didn't know anything. That's not quite true, because Dickie does do some gardening, but Paul knew so much more about it and would have supported the idea of self-sufficiency.'

As a consummate professional, Paul took a serious interest in all the productions he worked on, but Tricia knows that her husband enjoyed *The Good Life* more than anything he had done before. 'From the very first morning, Paul adored going to rehearsals. Everyone gelled so well, which meant that recording the show was fun.' The warmth and friendship generated during the making of the series was not restricted to cast members. It extended to everyone associated with the show, including the production team – and partners, too, were welcomed into the fold. 'We'd take it in turns cooking a meal, with everyone congregating at one house. There was certainly a feeling of togetherness.'

But it was an anxious Paul Eddington who sat down to watch the first transmission of the show. 'He always felt nervous watching the first episode of anything,' remarks Tricia. 'He thought Richard and Felicity were lovely and the episode was all right, but he wasn't sure people would bother watching the second episode. He never took success for granted, especially as he knew you had to work hard to get it.'

Although *The Good Life* took a while to win over the viewers, all the characters became popular in their own right, as Paul's fan mail proved. 'He got letters from all sorts of people, including children who felt sorry for him because Margo kept putting him down. He couldn't go anywhere without people asking, "How's Margo?" He even had lorry drivers leaning out of the window and shouting down to him in the car.' Paul never minded being so closely associated with a character he had helped create – he ha'd spent too many years struggling in rep to worry

about that. 'Paul was always good about being recognized in the street, or replying to fan mail,' says Tricia. 'He said you didn't enter the business to be anonymous.'

Playing the henpecked Jerry Leadbetter launched Paul's TV career. From subsidiary characters and bit parts he was catapulted into the leading actor bracket, with a jam-packed diary the result. Often he would be working on stage in the West End at the same time as filming the series. After rehearsing at the Beeb during the day, he would grab a bite to eat before heading off for the theatre. It was a hectic schedule that could not go on indefinitely, but Paul was disappointed when *The Good Life* came to an end, as Tricia Eddington relates. 'He loved the show, and although he understood that it had to end some time, he still missed it when it did. But as the show became more and more successful, and the actors increasingly in demand, it was more and more difficult to get the four of them together at the same time.'

Shortly after finishing in *The Good Life* Paul was appearing in the West End in Alan Ayckbourn's *Ten Times Table* – the first play in which he had shared top billing – when John Howard Davies sent him the

pilot script of a new sitcom, *Yes, Minister,* written by Jonathan Lynn and Antony Jay. Although he was enthusiastic about the idea and liked the script, Paul wasn't sure that a sitcom about politics would appeal to the public. He asked to see further scripts and seriously considered rejecting the part, although he later admitted that he would have deeply regretted such a decision.

The 1980s was an extremely busy and rewarding decade for Paul, on both stage and TV. As well as three series of *Yes, Minister*, he recorded, amongst other things, seventeen episodes of the sequel, *Yes, Prime Minister*, two series of Thames' sitcom *Let There Be Love*, playing confirmed bachelor Timothy Love, the TV film of *Outside Edge* and radio adaptations of *Yes, Minister*.

With hit sitcoms like *The Good Life* and *Yes, Minister* being shown around the world, Paul became an international celebrity and was frequently invited to attend functions abroad on the strength of his small-screen successes. So widespread was the popularity of Lynn and Jay's political sitcom that Paul was mobbed by fans while on a visit to Turkey, having been invited there by the prime minister. Later that year he was greeted with an equal degree of warmth

WORKING WITH PAUL EDDINGTON

A TRIBUTE FROM **SYDNEY LOTTERBY**, DIRECTOR/PRODUCER
OF *YES, MINISTER* AND *YES, PRIME MINISTER*

When I first met Paul Eddington he had already become quite famous. When speaking to you, he chose his words carefully. He seemed slightly aloof, never off-guard. As a result, for me he never became easy to get to know.

He was a polite, gentle person – a gentleman, and a Quaker. His conversation was dotted with a fund of theatrical stories, which he'd willingly share. Given to a little pride at times, and perhaps even a little haughty, he enjoyed the fame of being the TV Prime Minister and the opportunities it gave him.

He was easy to work with and, even with all his experience in the theatre, never demanded to have his own way. He was a theatrical actor with a capital A, and proud of being in the 'profession'. I think he saw himself in the role of one of the knights of the theatre, which I've no doubt he would have become had this not been cruelly denied him by an untimely death.

His actorish manner was amply demonstrated to me on the occasion of my first *Yes, Minister*. After the last rehearsal of the day there's a break, when the engineers fix things and the lighting guys make final adjustments. It's possibly an hour before the audience are let in and is a time when most actors sit quietly, going over their various problems. Having

given them some last-minute notes, I tend to leave the cast alone, feeling they need this time to themselves. I remember being summoned to Paul's dressing room. Fearful of some awful thing I'd done, or not done, I entered his room only to be greeted genially with 'Sydney, dear boy, would you like a glass of sherry?' We talked not about the programme but about how I'd got into the BBC and whether I thought the series was good – all manner of subjects totally irrelevant to the imminent programme itself.

Paul's experience in his many comedy roles on stage had endowed him with a gift for comedy timing, which he used to great effect. During the whole run of *Yes, Minister* and *Yes, Prime Minister* there was a constant debate about whether there should or shouldn't be an audience. Sides were taken, with Nigel Hawthorne firmly against. I think so as not to rock the boat, Paul agreed it would be better not to have this distraction. Secretly, though, I think he welcomed the boost the audience gave him when he delivered a funny line to his satisfaction.

In all the time I worked with Paul, which must have been six years, I never once heard him complain about his disabilities. He would just dismiss them with a wave of his hand and blame it on his age.

when opening a new cultural centre in Israel for the British Council.

Offers of work continued to flood in, but by now Paul Eddington had reached the stage in his career where, for once, he could afford to be a little more selective about what he took on. However, although his professional fortunes were on the ascendant, his health was causing increasing concern. For many years Paul had suffered from a skin condition and

this was eventually diagnosed as mycosis fungoides, the skin cancer that led to his death in 1995 at the age of 68.

On that sad November day the entertainment world lost one of its most popular and best-loved actors. Friends, family and fellow professionals rallied round to help Tricia in her hour of need, among them the other cast members of *The Good Life*. 'They've been wonderful since Paul's death,' she says.

'They're all so kind and generous, I don't know what I would have done without them. Penelope is a very strong person and has been such a help. And so has Felicity. When I was with Paul in hospital, she, like the others, would visit. Once she brought a little hamper for me, and inside was a flask of coffee, a tiny box of chocolates, some sandwiches and a book of poetry. It was so thoughtful. They're so kind, they keep in touch, which is a legacy from Paul.'

Not long after Paul met Richard Briers back in 1972, when they were both sitting on the council of the actors' union, Equity, the two became close friends. 'He's still one of my dearest friends,' Tricia says of Briers. 'Every ten days or so he'll ring to find out how I am, and we see each other frequently. He's an absolute dear.'

Paul was appearing with Richard Briers in the West End right up until his final days. For years they had talked about working together again, and when Paul suggested David Storey's play *Home*, originally performed by theatrical knights John Gielgud and Ralph Richardson in 1970, Richard agreed it was a good choice.

Even though Paul was very ill by this time, he was determined to see the project through, as Tricia explains. 'I didn't know if he was well enough to do it, but it was a play he'd always wanted to do. It was a difficult time for him, but I'm sure he would have died sooner if he'd stopped working and given in to the illness. I'm glad that he kept going as long as he could.'

Thanks to repeats, new generations of television viewers can still enjoy the skill and professionalism of Paul Eddington – all four series of *The Good Life* have recently been re-run on the satellite channel UK Gold. Tricia Eddington believes that the sitcom retains a certain relevance. 'When you watch it now and see the boys with long sideburns and curly hair, and the girls – especially Margo – wearing up-to-the-minute clothes, it all seems so old-fashioned. But that doesn't really matter, because the whole idea of self-sufficiency is a theme that's still with us.'

ESMONDE ON EDDINGTON

With me, it's not a case of going for the 'rag-bag' look – I actually *am* a rag-bag. Whereas with Paul Eddington it was a case of his actually being a suave devil.

Paul would turn up for the read-through of *The Good Life* looking as though he'd just stepped out of the pages of a classy clothing catalogue. I've seen him in a suit – we all have, so you'll know what I mean – but his casual wear was the thing. I hope I'm not insulting his trousers by calling them 'quietly jazzy', but they're the sort of trousers that Paul would casually wear, along with casually matching, possibly mustard-coloured, woollens.

He would sit at the table along with the rest of us – his coffee *never* spilling – and you'd hear a couple of quiet, well-oiled clicks as he opened his slim and moody briefcase. Then he'd be ready. As a matter of fact, for every show he would have been ready for quite some time, because it now became manifest that he'd already put in a considerable amount of work on the words. They would fall from his mouth with a polished grace that made us writers smile contentedly.

That's what Paul was for me – an elegant and highly talented professional. His place in the world of acting is now occupied by a big hole.

PENELOPE KEITH

MARGO LEADBETTER

Margo is a kind-hearted snob, who buys her clothes from upmarket boutiques in London's Bond Street while complaining that her clothing allowance is too small. Thanks to her husband's well-paid job in the plastics industry, she lives a life of luxury to the point of extravagance. Her spendthrift manner sees her splashing out £70 on an outfit just for looking after the Goods' animals, intending to donate the clothes to the needy once her neighbours return from their much-needed weekend break.

While her husband works, Margo stays at home, supposedly looking after the house. But, as Jerry points out, Mr Pearson maintains the garden three times a week and the house is cleaned daily by Mrs Pearson. For all her shortcomings, Margo, with her A-level in domestic science, is the driving force behind her husband's success. She accepts all the

responsibility that go with being the wife of an up-and-coming executive and supports him all the way.

Apart from spending money, Margo has several other hobbies. She's a 'leading light' in the local music society, enjoys horse riding and is an active member of the Surbiton Ladies' Conservative Association. But despite being outwardly gregarious and giving every impression of being the bedrock of the household, she lacks self-confidence, perhaps as a result of a childhood in which she was constantly the butt of the other kids' fun. Her inability to understand jokes or let her hair down – something that has followed her into adulthood – earned her the nickname 'Starchy'.

Although not everyone's cup of tea, the outspoken Margo is always kind and generous towards the people who matter to her: her husband and close friends Tom and Barbara.

In 1977 Pye Radio & Television declared Penelope Keith the 'Funniest Girl of the Year' for her role in *The Good Life*, which was quite an achievement when you consider that her character was not even seen in the initial episode. Largely unknown as a television actress when she first adopted the haughty tones of Margo Leadbetter, Penelope quickly impressed her own inimitable style on the character and in no time at all the critics were lauding her performances.

Writing in the *Radio Times* in 1977, Julian Mitchell noted that, as the series progressed, the Goods 'gradually become the foils of the Leadbetters or, rather, of Margo'. He felt that, as viewers, we don't just 'laugh at Margo and her pretensions, we admire her – and more deeply than perhaps we know'.

Richard Briers agrees that Penelope's portrayal of the uppity Margo was a major factor in the sitcom's popularity. 'Penny was brilliant,' he enthuses. 'Her input was vital to the success of the show. I reckon we would have had several million less viewers if we'd had just an adequate actress, rather than a marvellous actress like Penny.'

When Margo and her husband Jerry were conceived by the writers, they were intended more as subsidiary characters (after all, someone had to suffer the eccentricities of the Goods). No one foresaw just how powerful Margo would become. But as the series bedded down and the characters began establishing themselves, it became clear that it would be possible to make more of the Leadbetters, especially Margo. Richard Briers recalls the time when the writers started doing just that. 'I remember when Bob and John decided to build up the character. They actually asked me, "Is it all right with you if we write her up?" and I replied, "Yes, write her up, she's dynamite!" It was the best role Penelope had ever had, and she played it beautifully.'

As with all good sitcoms, the success of the scripts relied upon drawing humour from the situation instead of just churning out a stream of one-liners. From the situation came the conflict, a cardinal ingredient in sitcoms, which paved the way for Margo to flourish. It was something that Brian Jones, the production assistant, had pleasure in witnessing. 'The conflict between the people created the humour, and Margo's reaction to it all, in particular, developed wonderfully.' Brian acknowledges that the character became strong enough to carry her own subplots. 'Margo was always fighting her corner against all sorts of bad workmen, for example. She was the "silent majority" and the writers saw this as something they could exploit to the benefit of the series.'

Even though it was *The Good Life* that turned Penelope Keith into a household name, she was already an established theatre actress, with over fifteen years' experience to her name. The ease with which she crossed mediums to portray the snooty Margo, with her patrician tones and snobbish attitudes, signified a bright TV future for the actress, who went on to win many awards, including the Variety Club of Great Britain's 'Show Business Personality of the Year', five *TV Times* awards and a BAFTA 'Best Light Entertainment Performance' award, twice. She has

As soon as Penelope left school she decided to pursue an acting career, a decision that came as no surprise to her mother and stepfather. 'I enjoyed appearing in plays at school, for which I was always cast in the leading parts because of my height,' recalls Penelope. But her dreams of becoming an actress received a temporary setback when she was rejected by the Central School of Dramatic Art – for being too tall! As RADA was too expensive, Penelope

also won several awards for her theatrical work, such as the Society of West End Theatres' award for 'Best Comedy Performance' in *Donkey's Years*.

Born in Surrey in 1940, Penelope spent her early years with her mother after her parents' marriage broke up when she was a baby. Her father served in the army during the war and had risen to the rank of major by the time he was demobbed. Since money was short, her mother, Connie, had to go out to work, which meant that, at the age of only six, Penelope was sent to boarding school in Seaford. Luckily, she enjoyed her days as a boarder, and in the summer holidays she would be reunited with her mother, who worked as a hostess in a Clacton hotel during the holiday season. Her mother remarried in 1950, at which point Penelope adopted her step-father's name of Keith.

applied to join the Webber Douglas Academy. She was lucky enough to be accepted and spent two years at drama school, earning much-needed cash in the reception office of London's Hyde Park Hotel in the evenings.

Upon graduation she began her professional career working in rep around the country and received her first wage packet of £7.50 at Chesterfield. She appeared in plays including *The Tunnel of Love* and played the mother in *Gigi* and the daughter in *Flowering Cherry*. Learning one's trade in repertory means mucking in and playing an assortment of different characters – invaluable experience for any thespian. Reflecting on that period of her career during an interview with *The Times*, Penelope said, 'Then came a whole series of Cockney whores in courtroom dramas, for which I had to dye my hair

red because they couldn't afford to hire me a wig. I was working sixteen hours a day… and loving every minute of it.'

Spells at Lincoln, Manchester and Salisbury reps followed, but her first important opportunity came in 1963 when she joined the Royal Shakespeare Company at Stratford and the Aldwych Theatre, London.

At this point her television appearances had been few and were limited to minor roles such as Primrose, the army librarian, in *The Army Game,* a physiotherapist in *Emergency – Ward 10* and a small part in an episode of *Hadleigh.* However, after a return to repertory theatre at Cheltenham she was cast in her first leading role on the small screen. Granada TV's *Six Shades of Black* was a series of hour-long plays, transmitted in 1965, in which the hero of one play

became the victim of the next. Penelope appeared as Lady Pandora Brewster in the play *There is a Happy Land,* acting alongside Pamela Brown and Peter Bull.

Although theatre remained her primary source of employment, her appearances on TV became more frequent, including roles in Yorkshire's drama *Kate* (starring Phyllis Calvert in her first TV series), *The Pallisers, Two's Company,* a TV production of *Private Lives* and a small-screen adaptation of Ayckbourn's *The Norman Conquests* for Thames in 1977, with Richard Briers playing her husband.

Penelope Keith was so successful as Margo in *The Good Life* that she became a household name almost overnight, which led to one of the busiest periods of her working life. At one point she was working 16-hour days, filming the sitcom and also appearing on stage in Michael Frayn's *Donkey's Years* at the Globe.

Penelope Keith's fine portrayal of the snobbish Margo
was a key factor in the sitcom's success.

It was also an important juncture in her small-screen
career, because she started being offered lead roles,
beginning with Audrey Fforbes-Hamilton in *To the
Manor Born*. Running to twenty-one episodes between
1979 and 1981, this sitcom achieved huge viewing
figures, the final episode being watched by almost
24 million people.

Originally intending the programme as a radio
series, featuring Penelope and Bernard Braden, creator
Peter Spence eventually adapted the idea for TV.
'Penelope is very professional,' comments Peter, who
had studied *The Good Life* scripts while learning the
craft of sitcom-writing. 'She's also a great leader,

inspiring confidence in people, as well as being easy
to work with. We often had plot discussions about
who should end up on top during a particular
episode – Audrey or Richard DeVere – because it was
always a battle between the two protagonists. But
she'd say it didn't matter who wins, we'll play it for
real. Some you lose, some you win. And that's what
happened. She was very much the star of the show and
one might have thought she should have the upper
hand all the time, but she didn't see it that way.'

To the Manor Born was produced by Gareth
Gwenlan, one of the BBC's senior producers, who
holds nothing but fond memories of working with
Penelope. 'It was the first time I'd worked with her,
and over the three-year period we shot the series, we
became good friends. As far as Penny's work as an
actress is concerned, she's hugely professional and has

all the attributes you expect from top performers – they're always on time, they're committed, they know their lines and they lead by example. Penny is the embodiment of that.

'You don't always get talent combined with absolute professionalism, but you do with her, and that makes life very easy. If your top star behaves properly, you don't get problems with anyone else, and consequently *To the Manor Born* was a pleasant experience. Years of training in the theatre made her a superb player in front of an audience, particularly in comedy, where her timing is perfect.'

Although some people have drawn a comparison between the role of Margo Leadbetter and that of Audrey Fforbes-Hamilton, Gareth did not feel there were any similarities.

'Margo was very "nouveau-riche" suburban, the first generation who'd made it, whereas Audrey Fforbes-Hamilton came from a family who'd been living in the manor house for 400 years, which is totally different. While Audrey's accent was genuine, and what you would expect from someone with her background, Margo had obviously "acquired" her way of speaking. Anyway, Margo was a terrible snob, whereas Audrey didn't need to be, because she really was upper class. She had certain dislikes, but that wasn't snobbery.'

By the time Penelope played Caroline Fairchild in ITV's 1986 sitcom *Executive Stress*, for which she won a Best Actress award, she was one of the country's top performers in the field of television comedy, and yet writer George Layton initially had difficulty imagining an actress like Penelope playing the female lead. 'It was about a woman who'd lost her confidence and forgotten just how talented she was before embarking on raising a family. It was a woman rediscovering her own confidence, whereas Penelope is very confident. But it was silly, thinking like that, and of course she was brilliant. She's a great technician and brought something extra to the part.'

When producer John Howard Davies read the script for *Executive Stress*, he instantly saw Penelope playing Caroline, which surprised George. 'I thought he'd suggest someone who played more diffident characters, but of course you can't be blinkered like that – an actress is an actress. Penelope was marvellous, always word-perfect, which, as a writer, I appreciated. She was hard-working, had great comedy timing and never put a foot wrong.'

As soon as the show had got under way, George Layton starting writing specifically with Penelope in mind, which gave him a different perspective on shaping the character. 'I began picturing Penelope, with her particular delivery, whenever I was writing the scripts. It helped in developing the character's relationship with her husband, because I was able to imagine Penelope acting the part. I could project a certain tone by writing lines which I knew she'd deliver well.'

story of 'an incompetent woman with no maternal instincts having no choice but to become a mother to her grandchildren, fighting every inch of the way.' The first of three series was transmitted in 1995, with William Gaunt playing Andrew Prentice and Penelope as his wife, Maggie.

The show was not written with Penelope Keith in mind, as co-writer Jan Etherington explains. 'A fellow writer was already working on a project for her at the time, so we deliberately didn't target her because we

They may have been as different as chalk and cheese, but the Goods and the Leadbetters were friends of long standing.

Executive Stress and an earlier sitcom, *Moving,* in which Penelope had played Sarah Gladwyn for just one series, began a long association with Thames Television. This went on to include chairing a new run of the game show *What's My Line?* in 1988, hosting her own gardening show, *Growing Places with Penelope Keith,* a year later, and appearing in two further sitcoms, *No Job For A Lady* and *Law and Disorder,* both written by Alex Shearer. When her next big success came along a year later in the shape of *Next of Kin,* it seemed as if Penelope had been everpresent on our screens since Margo, two decades earlier. Yet her busy TV schedule had not prevented her from continuing with her stage career.

The BBC sitcom *Next of Kin* is described by Jan Etherington, who created it with Gavin Petrie, as the

thought she'd be busy, although the other project didn't work out in the end. We wrote the series with Diana Rigg in mind, because we'd heard she was looking for a project in comedy at the time. But when Penny became free and her name was suggested, we thought she was perfect because she had all the qualities we wanted.

'We had to be brave with *Next of Kin.* We made sure it was a black comedy and didn't make any compromises with Penny's character. She had to be someone who hadn't liked being a mother when bringing up her own children, and certainly didn't want to be a grandmother having their children to look after. There are very few actors in the country who could have got that over to the public without being hated, but Penelope was one of them. The critics riled against her a bit, but the public loved her character, and *Next of Kin*.'

Jan Etherington believes Penelope Keith is at her best when she reveals a trace of vulnerability. 'In *Next of Kin* that showed in her inability to express the emotions she started feeling towards her grandchildren, and her feeling of hurt when they showed a preference for Bill Gaunt's character. Penny's a very powerful actress with a tremendous screen presence. She played her part beautifully.'

Gareth Gwenlan, who had previously worked with Penelope on *To the Manor Born*, was given the job of producing the series. From the moment he read the pilot script, he felt she was right for the part. 'I spoke to her and asked if she minded playing a grandmother,' he smiles. Penelope asked to see the scripts, and as soon as she read them she loved the character. 'The fact that she was playing a grandmother never bothered her. And anyway, by then Penny would have been in her mid-50s, so it was perfectly feasible for her character to have had grandchildren at that age.'

Gareth was, once again, pleased with how Penelope developed the character. 'It was a very difficult part to play – a grandparent who didn't like her own grandchildren, or her son and daughter-in-law. But it was very honest, and I thought Penny brought a great deal of warmth and fun into it. It did well.'

Next of Kin was an interesting project, in which the catalyst of the situation was the death of the main characters' son and daughter-in-law. For some people, trying to generate comedy from such a premise would seem almost impossible, but with the writing of Etherington and Petrie, and Gwenlan's direction, the show became a success. However, it was no doddle, as Gareth Gwenlan points out. 'We had to be careful, especially when breaking the convention whereby all grandparents are supposed to adore their grandchildren. Clearly there are some who don't, and we decided to be honest about this.'

Even though Penelope Keith is strongly associated with formidable roles like that of Margo, her adaptability and the ease with which she can turn her hand to any number of roles is unquestionable – not surprising, when you consider that in her RSC days in the early 1960s she was called upon to play anything from a crook to a tree!

LARBEY ON KEITH

When we were casting the part of Margo in *The Good Life*, John and I, to our eternal shame, suggested 'the actress in the Benson and Hedges commercial'! Penny Keith was, of course, already a very established stage actress, but all we'd seen of her was that wonderfully wrinkled nose in the ad as she smelt a whiff of cigarette smoke. I'm sure Penny was approached without any mention of this, and how lucky we were to get her.

On the surface there were so many things about Margo *not* to like. She was a huge snob, ultra-fastidious, quick-tempered and politically just to the left of Adolf Hitler. But we wanted her to be liked in spite of all this. So we inserted vulnerability, and how well Penny portrayed it. Beneath Margo's iron façade was a woman who was a loyal, if critical, friend, and one who was painfully aware that she was the butt of many jokes that she didn't even understand!

Margo, of course, passed into legend as the champion of 'the silent majority', though she was very seldom silent for long. Perhaps the hardest thing that Penny Keith had to do was play an essentially humourless character when she herself was great fun to work with. I believe it's called acting.

REGINALD MARSH

'SIR' ANDREW

When the sitcom begins, the cigar-puffing 'Sir' Andrew, married to Felicity, is managing director of JJM Ltd. An ex-military man and a stern authoritarian, he barks his commands and expects everyone to come running. But he has trouble with names – especially in the case of Tom, whom he invariably calls Tim. 'Sir' is an unreasonable and exacting taskmaster, a character flaw compounded by the bunch of lapdogs he employs. By the time we wave goodbye to life in The Avenue, he has retired from the helm of JJM and bought a 200-acre manor house in Devon, formally owned by Viscount Plymouth, where he intends trying his own luck at self-sufficiency.

Reginald Marsh enjoys playing humourless characters – something he's done often during his career. One such role was that of Sir Dennis Hodge in *Terry and June*, which he adopted immediately after the final episode of *The Good Life*. 'They're fun to play, and "Sir" in *The Good Life* was one of my manic chairman types.' Playing the managing director of JJM was one of his favourite roles, and one of the things he remembers most was the air of geniality surrounding the show. 'Everyone was lovely to work with, and the cast was so inventive.'

One particular moment he remembers well involved Paul Eddington in the episode 'Mutiny'. Jerry is sacked for refusing to accommodate a Dutch

business associate who's visiting JJM, but when the Goods help persuade 'Sir' to change his mind, Jerry ends up speaking to him on the phone to invite him round for dinner. 'Just before he picks up the receiver, Jerry combs his hair. I thought that was brilliant, a stroke of genius.'

When it comes to playing authoritarian characters, Reginald relies on his own experiences in life, although he's quick to point out that he's nothing like them in real life. 'They were an amalgamation of different people I'd known, people in power. My character in *The Good Life* and Sir Dennis were very similar types and I felt they'd both come out of the services. I saw "Sir" as an air force man, probably finishing his time as a station commander. He was used to ordering people around and getting his own way, with nobody answering back. Then he set up JJM making ridiculous plastic toys for cereal packets, but still treated his workforce like squaddies.'

Reginald regards himself as an intuitive actor, never worrying too much beforehand about how to play a particular role. 'You get lines given to you and you simply play them. As my character was the straight man, I had to play the lines to help show off the comic actor – either Richard Briers or Paul Eddington – to his best advantage.'

In all, Reginald appeared in six episodes, including the first, 'Plough Your Own Furrow'. Recording a new series in front of a studio audience is never easy, and, as he remembers, *The Good Life* was no exception. 'When you record a new show, the audience is usually one that really wanted to see something else. They write to the ticket department hoping to see a current show, only to be told it's not being recorded any more, but there are tickets for a new one if they'd like those instead. So people turn up knowing nothing about the new show, and then they see the main characters, none of whom they've met or heard of before, and it's very difficult at first.'

Until the audience appreciates the characters, and understands the basis of the sitcom's humour, there is often a lack of laughter, which is what Reginald remembers during the recording of episode one. To help the audience along, some of the early scenes were repeated during the recording. 'In the scenes where Tom Good is complaining about being forty and then finds out he's been left out of the department's cricket team, the audience didn't laugh much. In these circumstances, audiences usually find it funnier the second time around, so we did the scenes again. That way, people have already heard the dialogue and don't have to concentrate quite so hard in case they miss something, which frees them up to laugh at whatever they think is funny.'

After the first recording, members of the cast and crew assembled in the BBC bar, where, as Reginald Marsh noticed, everyone was a little disconsolate. 'I don't think anyone thought the episode had gone down very well,' he says. 'We thought we'd finish the first series, because we'd been contracted, but that would be it. No one was a particularly happy bunny. But then, of course, it took off and became a cult.'

Although he was born in London, in 1926, Reginald spent his early years in Worthing. After leaving school, he joined a bank. 'My father got me the job, because he thought it was a good idea for me to have a steady career.' But deep down Reginald knew that his long-term future lay elsewhere, and over time his interest in amateur dramatics took on a greater importance. With the help of his father, Reginald was introduced to a retired actress who lived locally. 'There was no history of acting in my family, but my father was very helpful. He was a kind, gentle man, and once he knew I was serious about wanting to act, he helped as much as he could.'

Reginald met the retired actress and her husband, who in turn introduced him to an agent they knew, who was helping the local repertory company in Worthing. Their meeting went well and shortly afterwards Reginald was hired as a juvenile in a production of J. B. Priestley's *Eden End*. 'I was about sixteen at the time, and must have been good enough because I was kept on,' says Reginald. 'Then I worked for the famous Harry Hanson's Court Players, up and down the country at various repertory companies. From then on, I was fortunate to stay in work, and because I wasn't fit enough to join the forces, I continued working in the theatre, gaining valuable experience.'

Years of theatre work around the country followed, but in 1958 Reginald put away the greasepaint for a while and joined the staff of Granada Television, working behind the scenes. 'I got a part in a tour of *Teahouse of the August Moon*, which lasted about ten months,' he recalls. 'It was a lovely show, but afterwards I became a little disillusioned. I parted company with my agent and just decided to take a break from acting.' The assistant stage manager who had auditioned Reginald for the part in *Teahouse* had started working for Granada, assisting the Head of Light Entertainment. Hearing that Reginald had quit the profession, he contacted him about a vacancy. 'He was looking for someone to run the department that finds contestants for quiz shows, like *Spot the Tune* and *Criss Cross Quiz*,' says Reginald, who was subsequently offered a six-month contract in Manchester.

After that period his contract was not renewed, but the contacts he had established at the station paid dividends in the form of his

TV debut. 'One of the directors I became friends with asked what I was going to do, and when I explained that I was returning to acting, he offered me a part in an episode of… no, I can't remember the show, but it turned out to be my debut.'

Reginald's next job on TV, in an episode of *Murder Bag*, quickly followed, and although he continued to appear on stage, spending periods with the RSC and the National Theatre, he preferred working on television. 'I've always been a home person and don't enjoy scampering around the country on tour. Jobs on television are also over quickly. You may have to go away, but it's usually just for a couple of weeks and then it's finished. I enjoy the theatre, and it's lovely to go on and get the laughs, but television comedy is just as challenging.'

In a career spanning five decades, Reginald has worked in all areas of the profession. He has a handful of film credits and was seen in 1962's *The Day the Earth Caught Fire*, *The Sicilians* (1963), *Shadow of Fear* (1963), *Material Witness* (1965) and *Berserk!* (1967).

On TV he is best known for his comedy roles in shows such as *Terry and June* and *George and Mildred*, but he also did lengthy stints in ATV's drama *The*

Plane Makers (which spotlighted the aviation industry, with Reginald playing the general works manager) and long-running soaps *Crossroads* (as garage-owner Reg Lamont) and *Coronation Street*. As bookie Dave Smith, Reginald appeared in the *Street* intermittently between 1962 and 1976, even though the part was only expected to last for two episodes. His character eventually left to run a country club.

Nowadays Reginald lives in retirement on the Isle of Wight. With his wife, Rosemary, he spends much of his time supporting the Isle of Wight branch of MENCAP. 'We have a mentally handicapped son, who's now in his thirties. He has Down's syndrome and has recently gone into residential care. We're both very active with the local branch, which takes up a lot of time.'

Reginald crops up on our screens in repeats, but retirement has ruled out any new shows. 'I'm just very fortunate to live in such a wonderful place and be able to enjoy it,' he says contentedly.

EPISODE GUIDE

PRODUCTION TEAM

(Unless otherwise stated, the people mentioned performed the job throughout the show's life)

SCRIPTS: All scripts written by John Esmonde & Bob Larbey

MUSIC: Burt Rhodes

ANIMAL NOISES: Percy Edwards (Series 3, episode 1)

COSTUMES: Rita Reekie (Series 1 & 2); Janet Tharby (Series 2, episodes 1, 3, 4, 5 & 6); Sally Nieper (Series 3 & 4); Peter Shepherd (Royal Command Performance); Rupert Jarvis (Christmas Special)

MAKE-UP: Marianne Ford (Series 1, 3, 4 & Royal Command Performance); Jenny Shircore (Series 2); Jean Speak (Christmas Special)

FILM CAMERAMAN: Len Newson (Series 1, except episode 6; Series 2, episodes 1, 3, 4, 5 & 6); Ken Willicombe (Series 3, episodes 1, 2, 3, 4, 5 & 7; Series 4); Peter Hall (Royal Command Performance)

VISUAL EFFECTS: Peter Pegrum (Series 1, episodes 5 & 7; Series 3, episode 6)

FILM SOUND: Richard Boulter (Series 1, except episode 6); Barry Tharby (Series 2, episodes 1, 3, 4, 5 & 6); Jack Curtis (Series 3, episodes 1, 2, 3, 4, 5 & 7); Martyn Clift (Series 4); John Jellick (Royal Command Performance)

FILM EDITOR: Bill Harris (Series 1, except episode 6; Series 2, episodes 1, 3, 4, 5 & 6); Ian McKendrick (Series 3, episodes 1, 2, 3, 4, 5 & 7; Series 4); John Dunstan (Royal Command Performance)

PRODUCTION ASSISTANT: Brian Jones

TITLES: Oliver Elmes

COMMENTARY: Brian Johnston (Royal Command Performance)

LIGHTING: Ron Koplick (Series 1, 2, 3, 4 & Royal Command Performance); Fred Wright (Christmas Special)

SOUND: Laurie Taylor (Series 1 & Christmas Special); John Delany (Series 2 & 3); Mike Giles (Series 4); Michael McCarthy (Royal Command Performance)

DESIGNER: Paul Munting

PRODUCER: John Howard Davies

1: Plough Your Own Furrow

Original transmission: Friday, 4 April 1975, BBC1, 8.30pm

First repeat: Tuesday, 1 June 1976, BBC1, 9.25pm

Original viewing figures: 5.9 million

CAST

Tom Good	Richard Briers
Barbara Good	Felicity Kendal
Margo Leadbetter	
(heard but not seen in first episode)	Penelope Keith
Jerry Leadbetter	Paul Eddington
Sir	Reginald Marsh
Commissionaire	Norman Atkyns
Brian	Martin Neil

Tom Good has reached his fortieth birthday, but instead of celebrating, he's reviewing his priorities. The daily treadmill of battling through the rush hour to his hated job with JJM Ltd is getting him down, and it seems the ideal time for a change. Escaping the constant traffic jams and petrol fumes, and the futility of designing plastic toys as breakfast-cereal giveaways, appeals to him more and more – especially since being overlooked for the departmental cricket match on the grounds of his age and discovering that the new moulding he's expected to design is a giraffe!

Over a glass of wine with Barbara he weighs up the pros and cons of his life, and is still scribbling down his thoughts at three o'clock in the morning. Finally, he decides his destiny: he intends to break the vicious circle of relying on a mundane job to earn money. Tom presents his wife with the idea of their becoming self-sufficient and fending for themselves, but admits that many sacrifices will have to be made to achieve that goal, so it's not a decision to be taken lightly. Barbara mulls the proposition over in the garden, her private retreat whenever serious thinking is called for, and after careful consideration agrees that self-sufficiency in Surbiton could be a goer.

Early next morning Tom swaps his car for a garden rotavator and informs Jerry that he's kicking the habit of commuting. And when Barbara announces that their goat is due to arrive by midday, Jerry is left dumbfounded by his neighbours' crusade.

2: Say Little Hen…

Original transmission: Friday, 11 April 1975, BBC1, 8.30pm

First repeat: Tuesday, 8 June 1976, BBC1, 9.25pm

Original viewing figures: 8.2 million

NOTE Richard Briers, Felicity Kendal, Penelope Keith and Paul Eddington appear in all remaining episodes.

ADDITIONAL CAST FOR THIS EPISODE

Sir . . . . Reginald Marsh

Felicity (Sir's wife) . . . . Moyra Fraser

Jerry arrives home from work with two extra passengers – Tom and his goat, which he had been exercising on the local common – and when Barbara begins demolishing the greenhouse to convert it into a chicken shed, the Leadbetters' concern intensifies. While Margo voices her opinion that the residents' association should have been informed of the changes taking place next door, Jerry ponders whether Tom's quest for self-sufficiency is due to a nervous breakdown.

Although Tom and Barbara appear earnest about their new way of life, Margo fears they're heading for 'degradation, misery and squalor'. Jerry, meanwhile, is worried about the direction his ex-colleague's life is taking, regarding his obsession with self-sufficiency as no more than a fad. He aims to help Tom back onto the straight and narrow by inviting him and Barbara to dinner, together with 'Sir' Andrew, their boss at JJM, who Jerry hopes will offer Tom his old job back.

'Sir' is not keen on Jerry's idea – after all, he's 'running a company, not a psychiatric ward'. But when he hears that one of the company's major accounts may be in jeopardy without the services of Tom Good, he quickly changes his mind. However, Tom isn't interested in returning to work. Having finally freed himself from the burdens of office work, he's more than content with his new-found lifestyle.

3: The Weaker Sex?

Original transmission: Friday, 18 April 1975, BBC1, 8.30pm

First repeat: Tuesday, 15 June 1976, BBC1, 9.25pm

Original viewing figures: 6.5 million

ADDITIONAL CAST FOR THIS EPISODE

Sam . . . . Tony Selby

GPO Man . . . . Paul McDowell

When Tom salvages a rusty old range from the back of a rag-and-bone man's cart and gives Barbara the job of restoring it to pristine condition, she wonders whether a self-sufficient lifestyle was such a good idea after all. Reminders of their former life as comfortably-off middle-class citizens are rapidly being stripped away as they discard all non-essential items. When the man from the GPO comes to disconnect the phone, Margo misinterprets the situation, concluding that things must be really bad next door, and in an effort to help offers Barbara one of her old dresses. Barbara is far too proud to accept hand-me-downs, but Tom, with his frugal outlook, accepts the garment. To Margo's annoyance, it turns out that he doesn't want it for his wife, but for his newly-built scarecrow!

Barbara reaches boiling point when Tom enthuses over the virtues of self-sufficiency while she's getting dirtier and dirtier cleaning the range. Craving for a taste of 'civilization' again, she slips next door, covered in dirt and rust, and sinks two martinis. But it's not long before she feels sorry for her husband and returns home to enjoy a coffee with him in front of their sparkling new range.

Aware that the Goods are looking for something to keep the birds away from their newly planted seedlings, Sam, the Spanish villa-owning rag-and-bone man, drops in with the perfect solution: a little black kitten. The trouble is, the cat's keen on birds – but the wrong type, as Tom and Barbara soon discover when they catch him chasing their chickens round the garden.

4: Pig's Lib

Original transmission: Friday, 25 April 1975, BBC1, 8.30pm

First repeat: Tuesday, 22 June 1976, BBC1, 9.25pm

Original viewing figures: 7.9 million

ADDITIONAL CAST FOR THIS EPISODE

Mr Carter . . . . Robert Gillespie

Window Cleaner . . . . Jonathan Lynn

Mr Wilks . . . . Lionel Wheeler

Man . . . . John Lawrence

The Goods are getting into the swing of this self-sufficiency lark. While Barbara offers home-made wine and spring onions to the window cleaner, Tom pays for his copy of *Pig Breeder* and bag of potato peelings with eggs. When Margo discovers that Tom is collecting household scraps in preparation for expanding his livestock, beginning with pigs, she's horrified and dispatches Jerry to warn their neighbours against such a move. Unperturbed by Jerry's weak-willed threat of bringing Mr Carter, the new chairman of the residents' association, into the fight, the Goods introduce pigs to The Avenue.

Matters escalate and Mr Carter and Margo attend a meeting at the Goods' house, but things don't turn out as Margo had planned. Carter has an open-minded attitude and acknowledges that Tom's plan to convert dung into fuel is not such a bad idea. Margo, whose only remaining argument is fear of the pigs escaping and trampling over her garden, concedes defeat and storms off.

But it seems Margo's concerns were justified after all, as Pinky and Perky dig a hole under the fence and are found munching chunks out of the Leadbetters' treasured lawn. The pigs are soon heading for the slaughterhouse. It's a bitter disappointment for the Goods, but they're resilient and prepared to battle on. When Jerry becomes concerned that he and Margo will lose the friendship of their neighbours, Margo pops next door to stress that they want to remain chums. Tom and Barbara accept Margo's olive branch, but not before telling her how the ten-week-old piglets were sent away to die. They lay it on thick to make Margo feel culpable, so much so that she hands Tom her car keys and orders him to save the poor little creatures' lives. Margo is relieved when he returns with the two porkers, but what she doesn't know is that although the names are the same, the pigs are not!

5: The Thing in the Cellar

Original transmission: Friday, 2 May 1975, BBC1, 8.30pm

First repeat: Tuesday, 29 June 1976, BBC1, 9.25pm

Original viewing figures: 8 million

ADDITIONAL CAST FOR THIS EPISODE

Angler . . . . Ray Mort

Tom has been slaving away in the cellar all week, building a generator. When Jerry and Margo call round, he gives Jerry a demonstration of his mechanical masterpiece. A flick of the switch, a spin of the flywheel and the machine splutters into life – but not for long. It may need refinement! While Margo and Jerry worry about the impending power cuts, Tom glories in the assurance that, as long as he can lay his hands on enough pigs' manure, he'll have power to keep his house illuminated and warm.

Margo can't understand the Goods' display of delight when the generator is declared fully operational, especially when one of their armchairs starts to vibrate while it's running. She would rather rely on the National Grid and isn't worried one bit by Tom and Barbara's proclamation that at least they won't suffer when the power cuts take hold.

The next day Jerry invites Tom to join him in a round of golf or a spot of fishing. Tom says he hasn't the time, until Barbara points out the advantage of angling: free fish. Although the catch is small, Tom is pleased when they're able to stock their freezer with filleted fish.

After exerting themselves chopping the fish, the Goods head for the common and a little more chopping – this time wood. The local council have felled a large tree and allow Tom and Barbara to take as much wood as they like before it's removed. However, they're expecting an electrician, who's coming to check the standard of Tom's wiring, so they persuade Jerry to give up part of his Saturday to wait for him at their house. When the vibrating armchair stops shaking, Jerry realizes that the generator has packed up and breaks the news to the Goods on their return. Unable to buy a new intake valve until Monday, Tom and Barbara find the thought of two candlelit evenings quite appealing – but what about the frozen fish? They race next door to ask Jerry to keep them in his freezer, just as the power cuts begin.

6: The Pagan Rite

Original transmission: Friday, 9 May 1975, BBC1, 8.30pm

First repeat: Tuesday, 6 July 1976, BBC1, 9.25pm

Original viewing figures: 8.7 million

ADDITIONAL CAST FOR THIS EPISODE

Sir . . . . Reginald Marsh

Felicity (Sir's wife) . . . . Moyra Fraser

Waiter . . . . John Scott Martin

Jerry invites Tom and Barbara to dinner, but he has an ulterior motive. 'Sir' has specifically requested their presence, and as the fawning Jerry hates displeasing his boss, he pleads with the Goods to accept the invitation. Believing his ex-boss wants to give him his old job back, Tom is surprised to be offered freelance work, helping out with the company's forthcoming exhibition. Although Tom declines, 'Sir' makes sure he knows his home phone number and states that the offer is open until the weekend.

While chatting one evening, the Goods discuss what they miss about the old days, when life involved things like commuting – and money. What Barbara misses most are the times when they'd splash out and stay at a hotel. Feeling his wife deserves a little pampering again, Tom secretly pops next door to tell Jerry he's decided to take on the freelance work, on condition that it's kept from Barbara so that he can give her a pleasant surprise. Jerry offers Tom the use of his study, where he'll be able to work in peace and secrecy, or so they think. When Margo breaks into the desk and unearths Tom's work, she tells all to friend Barbara, only to be stunned by her reaction of disappointment and anger.

Barbara confronts Tom and flies into hysterics when he says he only did it for her, before both hitting and hugging him for being so 'bloody perfect'. The £200 Tom is paid for freelancing is spent on an overnight stay in a hotel bridal suite, a £50 dinner and a present for Barbara, while Jerry looks after the menagerie back home.

7: Backs to the Wall

Original transmission: Friday, 16 May 1975, BBC1, 8.30pm

First repeat: Tuesday, 20 July 1976, BBC1, 9.25pm

Original viewing figures: 7.7 million

ADDITIONAL CAST FOR THIS EPISODE

Doctor . . . . June Jago

George . . . . Billy Milton

Molly . . . . Pamela Manson

Ron, the Landlord . . . . Frank Lester

Harry . . . . Harry Goodier

While Margo and Jerry jet off to Kenya on holiday, Tom and Barbara are busy harvesting their crops, until tragedy strikes. Tom pulls the muscles in his back and is out of action for seven days. Their despair deepens when a stormy night wreaks havoc, leaving their garden looking like a bomb site. Unless the devastation is rectified within days, their whole year's harvest will have gone for a burton. To recruit helpers, Barbara heads for the local pub, but none of their so-called friends will lend a hand.

There's nothing Barbara can do but roll up her sleeves and do everything herself, and after a gruelling 14-hour day trudging around in the mud, she's shattered. With the rain still beating against the windows, Tom isn't proud of what he's putting his wife through and begins questioning the merits of self-sufficiency. But he sleeps on it and by the following morning his drive and positiveness are restored.

An eleventh-hour solution materializes when the Leadbetters return early from their holiday (Margo couldn't stand Africa) and are roped in to help save the harvest in Tom and Barbara's mudpit of a garden – despite the fact that Jerry's leg is in plaster as a result of a one-sided tangle with a Land Rover!

SERIES TWO

1: Just My Bill

Original transmission: Friday, 5 December 1975, BBC1, 8.30pm
First repeat: Thursday, 23 February 1978, BBC1, 7.40pm
Original viewing figures: 9.2 million

ADDITIONAL CAST FOR THIS EPISODE

Restaurant Owner	Wolfe Morris
Clerk	Frank Gatliff
Van Driver	Blake Butler
Woman	Ruth Kettlewell

To celebrate bringing in the harvest, Margo and Jerry are invited to dinner at Tom and Barbara's, the evening kicking off with a glass of home-made wine that's about as palatable as paraffin! It has certainly been a fruitful harvest, as produce occupies every spare nook and cranny in the Goods' house, even under the bed and in the chest of drawers. But Margo and Jerry doubt that Tom will find it as easy as he thinks to sell his produce and are surprised to hear that he has already won his first order – from a restaurant in town.

However, Tom's confidence is shattered when the sale falls through. While he was hoping for a one-off sale, the restaurant owner wants a guarantee of a year's supply, as he'd have to drop his regular supplier in order to take Tom's produce. Relenting slightly, the man offers Tom £70 instead of the £90 previously agreed, but Tom can't afford to sell at a reduced price and realizes he hasn't done his homework. He'll just have to find another buyer, even though that won't be easy.

Everywhere he tries to sell his vegetables Tom is rejected, and his depression deepens when Barbara shows him the final demand for the rates. Then suddenly he has a brainwave: he'll cut out the middle man and sell direct to the public. Even this scheme is doomed to failure, however. Barbara sells a mere two pounds of carrots from their stall in front of the house, while Tom sells hardly anything at all, trudging around the neighbourhood with his dilapidated pram. And to top it all, Ronnie Boxall, a mobile fruiterer and greengrocer who

has spent ten years building up his business, threatens Tom, accusing of him of trying to take away his trade.

Tom's despondency worsens as he begins to regret not devising a more successful strategy. He feels that they've planted the wrong crops, and that a better selection could have made all the difference. With only six days left until the rates are due, the Goods decide that their only option is to try and cover at least most of the £81.20 by selling their produce at a loss. Pulling out all the stops, they manage to scrape enough funds together by using the loose change left in the phone-bill box, retrieving coins from the back of chairs and exchanging a one-peseta note. Tom donates his very last penny to charity and feels on top of the world for doing so – until Barbara gets caught short and needs a coin for the loo!

2: The Guru of Surbiton

Original transmission: Friday, 12 December 1975, BBC1, 8.30pm
First repeat: Friday, 6 May 1983, BBC1, 7.00pm
Original viewing figures: 10.5 million

ADDITIONAL CAST FOR THIS EPISODE

Guy	Bruce Bould
Ruth	Irene Richards

When Jerry and Margo return from a few days in Amsterdam, they discover that Tom and Barbara have taken in two 20-year-old students, Guy and Ruth. In return for bed and board, the students are helping out around the place, doing odd jobs such as cleaning the cultivator. They are very earnest and before long begin worshipping the Goods, who they see as running a 'university of life'. Ruth takes a fancy to Tom and starts clinging to his every word. Both she and Guy want to be taught the Goods' philosophy.

The following day, just as Jerry arrives home at 6.30pm, Tom and Barbara are invited round to Margo's

In the episode 'The Guru of Surbiton', Tom finds himself elevated to iconic status in the eyes of two students who come to stay with him and Barbara.

for a meeting. The Turner's house, next door to the Goods', is up for sale and Margo wants to prevent any 'undesirables' purchasing the property. No one but Margo takes the meeting seriously and Tom sums up the general mood when he remarks that everyone should mind their own business.

Before the meeting closes, Guy comes knocking on Margo's French windows declaring his and Ruth's intention to establish a commune in the Goods' house. He wants to 'extend the concept' with Tom as a patriarchal figure. When Tom makes it clear that he's not interested, Guy says they'll have to put plan two into operation – that is, to buy the house next door. Tom and Barbara are no more keen on the idea than Margo and Jerry, but

they accept that it's still nothing to do with them and refuse to interfere.

Relief is felt all round when Guy and Ruth announce they'll be moving on after all. Ruth admits that she couldn't cope with living next door to Tom, the way she feels about him, and Guy has suddenly realized that he wants Ruth more than the commune. When the Leadbetters are given the news, Margo is so relieved that she cancels her plans to move to Cobham.

3: Mr Fix-It

Original transmission: Friday, 19 December 1975, BBC1, 8.35pm
First repeat: Thursday, 2 March 1978, BBC1, 7.40pm
Original viewing figures: 9 million

ADDITIONAL CAST FOR THIS EPISODE

Mr Coles . . . . John Quayle
Delivery Man . . . . Steve Emerson

Autumn has arrived and the nights are drawing in. Tom, who has been gardening in a dinner jacket, is anxious to make the most of the evenings, but this one is interrupted when Margo informs him that a Mr Coles, a reporter, wants him on the telephone. It turns out that the journalist intends writing an article about self-sufficiency, and a visit is arranged.

The following morning Margo sees Tom and Barbara being photographed in their garden. Knowing they're going to be featured in a newspaper article, she's keen to muscle in on the action, but Tom does his best to prevent this by going indoors. Mr Coles continues the interview, but it's not long before Margo is knocking on the door and controlling the conversation. The journalist isn't particularly interested in what Margo has to say, until the Goods start singing her praises, telling him how supportive she's been.

When Mr Coles calls to tell everyone he's sold the article to 'The Observer', Margo starts phoning all her friends to tell them to keep their eyes peeled for the article in next Sunday's edition. Spotting a chance for his hard-up friends next door to cash in on their fame by allowing their names to be used in advertising campaigns in return for freebies, Jerry takes care of the marketing and soon Tom and Barbara find themselves being showered with all sorts of gifts, including wine, bales of hay, new overalls, garden tools, even a small yacht.

But the article fails to appear in the following weekend's edition of *The Observer* and it turns out – to Jerry and Margo's horror – that the story was sold not to the national paper, but to the *Oxfordshire and Buckinghamshire Observer*.

4: The Day Peace Broke Out

Original transmission: Friday, 2 January 1976, BBC1, 8.30pm
First repeat: Thursday, 9 March 1978, BBC1, 7.40pm
Original viewing figures: 9.3 million

ADDITIONAL CAST FOR THIS EPISODE

Magistrate . . . . James Cossins
Harry Bennett (the thief) . . . . Brian Grellis

There's a thief in The Avenue. When Tom finds he's lost eight leeks from the front garden, he assumes someone is lifting them for their own table. When eight more are taken it's time for action, and he starts patrolling his garden at night. Catching the culprit looks unlikely, but just as Tom is ready to swap the cold, muddy garden for a warm bed, the phantom leek-pincher strikes. Tom gives chase and takes a pot-shot at the man with his airgun.

Just when Tom thinks he's seen the last of the thief, a summons drops through the letter box – he's been charged with assault. In court the thief is fined ten pounds and Tom is bound over for three months, the magistrate accepting that the loss of his leeks has obviously affected him more than it would a 'normal' man. But Tom, who never takes the easy route in life, states boldly that he can't promise to keep the peace, thus landing himself in prison for 28 days!

With her beloved hubby behind bars it's an upsetting time for Barbara, but his stretch as a jailbird is short-lived and after three days he's released. Back in The Avenue a 'Welcome Home, Scarface' card greets his return, and the champagne corks pop as Margo and Jerry join in the celebrations.

Once back home, Tom returns to his garden, only to find that the leek-thief has turned up in the hope of making peace. Understandably, at first Tom doesn't want to know, but when the culprit (whose name is Harry) explains that he lives in a high-rise flat, that taking the leeks was an aberration, and more importantly that one of his interests is cricket, Tom offers him a cup of tea. Before long the two men have become very pally, and Harry, a painter and decorator, offers to paint the outside of Tom's house as a way of making amends. When Harry leaves, Tom tells him to grab some leeks on the way out. But when Barbara, who has been out exercising Geraldine, the goat, comes down the road and spots him helping himself, unaware of what's been going on, she sets the goat on him!

5: Mutiny

Original transmission: Friday, 9 January 1976, BBC1, 8.30pm
First repeat: Thursday, 16 March 1978, BBC1, 7.40pm
Original viewing figures: 11.7 million

ADDITIONAL CAST FOR THIS EPISODE

Sir . . . . Reginald Marsh

Over a game of golf, which Jerry does his utmost to lose dismally for diplomatic reasons, 'Sir' asks Jerry if he'll put up a visitor from Amsterdam for the weekend. But Jerry has forgotten that this weekend is the highlight of Margo's social calendar, as she's starring in *The Sound of Music* at Surbiton Town Hall. When his wife refuses to provide hospitality for the Dutch visitor, he has the un-enviable task of breaking the news to his tyrant of a boss.

The consequences are dire: Jerry is summarily given a month's notice. Before he can think about job-seeking, however, he has to support his wife on her big night and attempt to calm her first-night nerves. At 42, he knows it won't be easy to find another post, and supplying food and drink for Margo's first- and last-night celebrations (on consecutive nights, as it's only a two-night run) is an expense he could do without just now. When Margo is the only one who comes back for the party, it looks as though there'll be a lot of waste. She admits that it was an awful show, thanks to exploding footlights, a boy with a runny nose, a conductor with a broken arm, and a decision by the Mayor to take the show off after the first night because it was harming the borough's reputation!

Even more upset about letting her husband down by showing him no sympathy about losing his job, Margo admits that she should have agreed to entertain the Dutch businessman. But Jerry will hear none of this and points out that the evening was important to her and the company doesn't own him. While Margo and Jerry slip off to bed, Tom hatches a plan to rescue his friend's job. The following day, over a glass of his pea-pod wine, he tries persuading 'Sir' to give Jerry another chance. These efforts seem to be heading nowhere, but then 'Sir' tells Tom and Barbara he acknowledges that he was too harsh and has already changed his mind – leaving them to pass on the good news.

It's not long before Jerry is crawling to the boss once again. Before picking up the phone to invite 'Sir', and his visitor, to dinner that weekend, he carefully combs his hair.

6: Home, Sweet Home

Original transmission: Friday, 16 January 1976, BBC1, 8.30pm
First repeat: Thursday, 23 March 1978, BBC1, 7.40pm
Original viewing figures: 12 million

ADDITIONAL CAST FOR THIS EPISODE

Mr May . . . . Edwin Brown
Mrs Weaver . . . . Charmian May

Margo pops round to let Tom and Barbara know that the new neighbours, Mr and Mrs Weaver, are just her cup of tea – they haven't a single paperback on their bookshelves, they hail from Bournemouth, they're staunch Tories and, what's more, they have a ceramic umbrella stand in their hallway. But she's alarmed to hear that the Goods have arranged for a boar to serve their pig, Pinky. Declaring that such things are not done in Surbiton, Margo storms out.

The following day, so determined is she not to be party to any of the sordid goings-on next door that she erects a shield to block out the view. After the event, Tom asks Mr May, the boar's owner, what he thinks of his and Barbara's efforts at self-sufficiency, and is taken aback when the man remarks that they're only playing at it. A country man himself, Mr May suggests that Tom should think of buying the eight-acre smallholding that's up for grabs near his place. Tom contemplates moving and, after visiting the site, admits he's all for it. When Barbara visits the Leadbetters to ask whether she can give their telephone number to the estate agent, she breaks down and confesses that she has no wish to move but can't pluck up the courage to tell Tom.

When Jerry calls on Tom to inform him that he's found a prospective buyer for the house, Tom, in turn, confides to his friend that he doesn't really want to leave, because the place is full of happy memories. Jerry thinks Tom should tell Barbara how he feels, but before he gets a chance, she blurts out her own feelings about the proposed move. Mightily relieved, Tom doesn't let on that he feels the same, but makes out that he's will-ing to sacrifice the smallholding for Barbara's sake. When Jerry spills the beans, eggs fly!

7: Going to Pot?

Original transmission: Friday, 23 January 1976, BBC1, 8.30pm

First repeat: Thursday, 30 March 1978, BBC1, 7.40pm

Original viewing figures: 12.2 million

ADDITIONAL CAST FOR THIS EPISODE

Mrs Weaver . . . . Charmian May

SERIES THREE

Tom and Barbara enrol for evening classes. They intend to do a house maintenance course together, with Tom also studying weaving and Barbara attending a pottery class. Since Margo is keen to try her hand at potting too, the Goods are assured of a lift each week.

Even before the first lesson, Margo is bitten by the pottery bug. With her birthday approaching, she persuades Jerry to invest in a state-of-the-art studio, fully kitted out with all the latest equipment. But her enthusiasm quickly wanes when she has a row with the tutor, which makes Jerry fume after he's spent so much money. Meanwhile, Tom and Barbara have decided that their respective classes are not for them, so they swap, with Tom transferring to the potter's wheel and Barbara to the loom.

On Margo's birthday Tom and Barbara give her a present – some attractive goblets that Tom has made at his evening class. When new neighbour Mrs Weaver, who is an artist, turns up to deliver the painting of Thames Ditton that she's completed for Margo, she takes an instant liking to the 'unfussy' goblets, which shocks everyone – not least Tom. He's dumbfounded when she asks him to make six more, and in no time this has led to further commissions. In order to keep up with demand and fulfil orders from Mrs Weaver's secretary and her friend with a lisp, Tom makes use of Margo's redundant equipment. It seems even better news when Margo announces that a friend of hers wants to sell Tom's goblets in her Chelsea studio – but when she proclaims that this means Tom and Barbara can soon be 'normal people again', it suddenly dawns on them that they're slipping away from their principles and it's time to put a stop to their commercial venture.

1: The Early Birds

Original transmission: Friday, 10 September 1976, BBC1, 8.30pm
First repeat: Thursday, 7 September 1978, BBC1, 8.00pm
Original viewing figures: 13.1 million

The Goods are out at the crack of dawn cultivating their garden, and waking the neighbours in the process. The Leadbetters are not happy, and when Margo demands the return of the nutcrackers she lent them back in 1967, Tom and Barbara realize they've offended her. They apologize and succeed in placating Margo, who relents and says they can keep the nutcrackers after all.

After a hard day's graft Tom and Barbara have managed to plant their seed potatoes, but they're daunted by the prospect of all the other tasks to be carried out if they're to achieve a bumper crop next year. Self-sufficiency is proving more difficult than they had anticipated. Tom wonders if their approach is wrong and suggests they make the most of the day by working throughout the daylight hours, not wasting a minute.

Attempting to change their sleep pattern, they go to bed early in preparation for getting up at sunrise, but, with Tom's puffing and Barbara's twitching, the experiment is not a great success. The next morning Barbara is overtired and snappy. The couple set about their work in the garden, trying, with difficulty, not to make any noise. However, it seems that their efforts at being neighbourly and considerate are being thrown back in their faces when they're awoken that evening by the sound of Des O'Connor's dulcet tones blaring out from the Leadbetters' party. They storm round in their dressing gowns to complain, but what they haven't realized is that it's only 8.30pm, so they accept Jerry's invitation and join the party — only to nod off on the sofa.

2: The Happy Event

Original transmission: Friday, 17 September 1976, BBC1, 8.30pm

First repeat: Thursday, 14 September 1978, BBC1, 8.00pm

Original viewing figures: 15.4 million

ADDITIONAL CAST FOR THIS EPISODE

Policeman . . . . George Innes

The Goods are expecting a baby – but the mother is Pinky, their pig. While they await the new arrival, Barbara believes she has resolved the problem of their lack of transport. Brian, an elderly white horse donated to them by Mr Betts, the coalman, seems an ideal replacement for Tom and Barbara's old cart, which Barbara has broken by sitting on it. However, Tom is not convinced that this is a viable proposition, since the cost of keeping the horse would probably outweigh any benefits.

Pinky goes into labour during the night and, while Barbara wakes Jerry to borrow his torch, Tom attends the birth. With Margo, Jerry and Barbara spectating, Tom delivers the eight piglets. But the last one born is a runt, and Tom plans to leave it to die – until an outcry from all the others forces him to change his mind. With the vet unavailable for another two hours, Tom (still in his dressing gown) drives Barbara and the baby pig to hospital in the hope that some oxygen will help. Things get complicated when they're pulled over by the police for speeding, but when Barbara explains the situation the boys in blue agree to co-operate.

Back in The Avenue, Tom constructs an oxygen tent for the little creature, but not before bullying Margo into bottle-feeding it. It's touch and go whether the piglet will make it as Tom places it inside the tent, but in the end their efforts are rewarded.

3: A Tug of the Forelock

Original transmission: Friday, 24 September 1976, BBC1, 8.30pm
First repeat: Thursday, 21 September 1978, BBC1, 8.00pm
Original viewing figures: 16.4 million

When the Leadbetters' gardener and cleaner, Mr and Mrs Pearson, take a month off visiting family in Canada, Margo and Jerry are left having to cut their own grass and do their own hoovering. Meanwhile, Tom and Barbara are contemplating how they'll cope

now that their only form of transport, a cart on wheels, is broken. One possible solution is to make a new vehicle using the cultivator engine with a bit of framework and a seat, but with only £1.28 in the bank they couldn't afford the fuel for it anyway.

When they pay a visit to Margo and Jerry, they find them arguing over the housework. Margo is finding it difficult having to scrub the floor herself. As the Leadbetters loathe housework and the Goods are strapped for cash, Tom and Barbara offer their services. Jerry jumps at the offer, and although Margo seems unhappy about ordering friends around, she soon has Barbara polishing the floor and cleaning the windows.

Barbara realizes that working for Margo is no doddle, and after a week of it she's tearing her hair out, fed up with constantly being told that Mrs Pearson cleans the corners better. Relations worsen when the Goods embarrass Margo in front of the Surbiton Ladies' Conservative Association, so she sacks them. Tom and Barbara can't help seeing the funny side of the affair, partly because the £22.50 they're owed in wages will be enough to run their newly-built vehicle for a whole ten months. But they hadn't reckoned on Jerry dropping the bombshell that if they plan to use their 'monstrosity' on the road, they'll have to pay tax and insurance. Needing more cash, they beg for their jobs back and are eventually given another chance.

Pleased to hear that Tom and Barbara have finally invested in some new transport, Margo suggests a lunchtime drink at the local pub. But when outside, she sees their rickety home-made vehicle and can't believe her eyes. Yet again embarrassed by her neighbours, she orders Jerry to drive on.

4: I Talk to the Trees

Original transmission: Friday, 1 October 1976, BBC1, 8.30pm

First repeat: Thursday, 28 September 1978, BBC1, 8.00pm

Original viewing figures: 16.7 million

ADDITIONAL CAST FOR THIS EPISODE

Mr Wakeling . . . . Noel Howlett

Mr Chipchase . . . . Raymond Mason

Madam Acting-Chairwoman . . . . Joyce Windsor

Down at the allotments Tom and Barbara discover Mr Wakeling talking to his plants. Over a cuppa, he claims that they respond to this treatment – after all, he says, they're alive too, and we should all live in harmony. Though initially sceptical, Tom gives some serious thought to what Mr Wakeling has said, especially as his own plants' welfare is so important. To test the idea, he conducts an experiment with his runner beans that involves Plant A being given 20 seconds of affectionate encouragement five times a day, Plant B being ignored altogether, and Plant C being exposed to derision and hatred for 20 seconds five times a day.

When the beans start growing, Barbara can't contain her excitement. Plant A, which she's named Douglas, is the biggest. To test out another of Mr Wakeling's theories, Tom digs out his old gramophone and 78s, planning to play music to the outdoor plants. But he couldn't have picked a worse time, because Margo is entertaining the local music society. An extraordinary meeting has been called, at which Margo (who had previously resigned) is poised to topple Miss Mountshaft, who many feel is a spent force, as president of the Society.

When Peter Dawson booms out of the gramophone, Margo feels her election campaign will be ruined, so she storms off to give the Goods a piece of her mind. But before she goes too far, Jerry breaks the good tidings that she has been elected president.

5: The Windbreak War

Original transmission: Friday, 8 October 1976, BBC1, 8.30pm

First repeat: Thursday, 5 October 1978, BBC1, 8.00pm

Original viewing figures: 15.8 million

ADDITIONAL CAST FOR THIS EPISODE

Mr Bailey . . . . Timothy Bateson

First workman . . . . Roger Pope

Second workman . . . . Desmond Cullum-Jones

To celebrate her appointment as president of the local music society, Margo plans to erect a windbreak. Concerned that it will cast a shadow over their newly planted fruits, Tom and Barbara invite Margo round. Tom plans to employ his charm to persuade Margo to reposition the thing, and although she sees through his compliments, she nevertheless agrees to do so.

The following morning Tom and Barbara notice the builders erecting the windbreak in the very same place. Surely Margo hasn't gone back on her word? As she is out, they set about resolving the problem by moving their fruit instead, exhausting themselves in the process. Unknown to them, when Margo arrives home and sees that the windbreak has not been placed where she instructed, she orders Mr Bailey, the builder, to move it.

When Tom and Barbara take a stroll in their garden that evening, they find the windbreak once again casting a shadow over their fruit. Enough is enough. Unaware that Margo was only sticking to her word by ordering the windbreak to be positioned as agreed, they demand an explanation. When she tells them what's happened, the Goods accept that they're in the wrong and apologize. To help patch things up, they pick up some home-made wine and dine at the Leadbetters' (even though they've invited themselves).

A jolly evening is had by all, and everyone gets a little tipsy. Before the evening is out, Jerry has admitted to Barbara that he fancies her, and lost the dishwasher, and Margo has confessed to Tom that she's not a complete woman as she's missing a sense of humour. However, she soon finds one when they decide to move the windbreak in the dark.

6: Whose Fleas are These?

Original transmission: Friday, 15 October 1976, BBC1, 8.30pm

First repeat: Thursday, 12 October 1978, BBC1, 8.00pm

Original viewing figures: 17.7 million

ADDITIONAL CAST FOR THIS EPISODE

Mr Bulstrode . . . . Michael Robbins

Postman . . . . Ray Dunbobbin

When tons of soot fall from the chimney, Tom and Barbara realize that a visit from the chimney sweep is long overdue. As the soot has put the fire out, there's no hot water for a bath, so they pop next door to use the Leadbetters' bathroom. While they're enjoying a drink in the hallway, Margo announces that she's been asked by Mrs Dooms-Patterson, wife of the local Conservative agent, to take an active part in Tory activities when the next election is called.

When the Goods arrive home it's not long before Barbara starts itching, and she becomes very depressed when Tom catches a flea. The next morning Tom decides to wash the animals in case they are the cause. It's important to clear up the problem before anyone finds out about it, but Barbara is worried: when they used Margo's bath, they could have passed the fleas on to their neighbours. Later, they ask Jerry and Margo whether they've been itching, too? When they say yes, Tom and Barbara break the news, which leaves Margo in hysterics.

When the council official arrives and explains that the source of the problem is a dog, the Goods are relieved – but they can't think of anyone who has a dog they've been in contact with. It turns out to be Ben, Mrs Dooms-Patterson's old English sheepdog. Jerry has the task of imparting this news to Margo.

7: The Last Posh Frock

Original transmission: Friday, 21 October 1976, BBC1, 8.30pm

First repeat: Thursday, 19 October 1978, BBC1, 8.00pm

Original viewing figures: 14.7 million

ADDITIONAL CAST FOR THIS EPISODE

Eileen . . . . Liz Robertson

Man in street . . . . Ronald Nunnery

Looking through some old photographs with Margo and reminiscing about their 1974 holiday in Scotland, Barbara is reminded of how smart she used to look. Margo admits that she used to be jealous of Barbara's dress sense, but certainly isn't now. Barbara feels she's losing her femininity, a fear that appears well founded when she ends up trying to repair the Leadbetters' car and, while pushing it down the road (for which Jerry promises to buy her a pint), gets mistaken for a boy. To top it all, she tears her only dress after slipping into it in an abortive attempt to get Tom to notice her for what she is – his wife, not a skivvy.

But her unhappiness doesn't go unnoticed by Tom. Knowing that Barbara's old schoolfriend Eileen, who's now living in Canada, is back in the country, he invites her to dinner, with Jerry and Margo making up the party.

On the evening of the party Barbara is no happier, particularly as she only has a dowdy old skirt and top to wear. Tom tells her he's not interested in all this 'tarting up' – it's the person that counts, not what they wear. But when the glamorous Eileen, who works as a model, walks in wearing a low-cut dress, Tom's eyes are on stalks all evening. This infuriates Barbara, who accuses him of being a 'two-faced rat'.

All Barbara wants is to feel like a normal, attractive woman again, and when Jerry chats with Tom the following day, he tries to tell him so. Realizing his mistake, Tom sells his watch in order to raise cash for a new dress. But he also has to sell his suit, so his attire for their meal with the Leadbetters consists of a dinner jacket and jeans!

SERIES
FOUR

1: Away from It All

Original transmission: Sunday, 10 April 1977, BBC1, 8.05pm
First repeat: Thursday, 2 November 1978, BBC1, 8.00pm
Original viewing figures: 7.5 million

Tom is not in the best of moods. He's been at the allotment picking his and Barbara's crop of vegetables, and the result of months of hard work is disheartening, with everything growing in miniature. There's hardly enough food to feed themselves, let alone any surplus for selling.

That evening the Goods have been invited to dinner with the Leadbetters, but Margo and Jerry quickly spot that Tom and Barbara are not their normal sparky selves. All attempts to cheer them up fail, and eventually Tom admits that life hasn't been very fair to them recently and they're fed up with it. Jerry suggests they take a break in a plush Mayfair flat, which he says won't cost them a penny. Robert, a friend of Jerry's who's out of the country, has offered the Leadbetters free use of his place while he's away. It's a nice thought, the Goods reply, but who would look after the animals? When Margo volunteers, Tom and Barbara can't believe their ears.

The Goods decide to take up this kind offer, but not before going over their plans, colour-coded diagrams and notes with Jerry umpteen times. He becomes annoyed at being treated like a child and shepherds Tom and Barbara out of the house into his car – something else they're borrowing.

Finally the couple head off, and before long they're lolling about watching *Kojak* and enjoying a decent alcoholic drink for once instead of home-made wine. Their Utopian lifestyle is interrupted by the phone ringing, and when it's Margo's voice they hear, panic sets in as they worry that something's gone wrong at home. Calm as ever, Margo explains that their generator has begun making a strange noise. After she's given Tom her impression of it, he diagnoses bearing trouble. Carrying out Tom's instructions, Jerry fixes the generator and everything is back to normal.

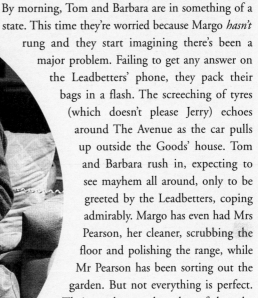

By morning, Tom and Barbara are in something of a state. This time they're worried because Margo *hasn't* rung and they start imagining there's been a major problem. Failing to get any answer on the Leadbetters' phone, they pack their bags in a flash. The screeching of tyres (which doesn't please Jerry) echoes around The Avenue as the car pulls up outside the Goods' house. Tom and Barbara rush in, expecting to see mayhem all around, only to be greeted by the Leadbetters, coping admirably. Margo has even had Mrs Pearson, her cleaner, scrubbing the floor and polishing the range, while Mr Pearson has been sorting out the garden. But not everything is perfect. Their mushrooms have been fed to the effluence digester!

2: The Green Door

Original transmission: Sunday, 17 April 1977, BBC1, 8.05pm

First repeat: Thursday, 9 November 1978, BBC1, 8.00pm

Original viewing figures: 15 million

ADDITIONAL CAST FOR THIS EPISODE

Mrs Holman . . . . Jane Hilary

Miss Harmsworth . . . . Toria Fuller

Tom and Barbara need 140 lbs of manure – and that's just for the front garden. While they're out trying to sort out their plight, Margo pulls up in her sporty green VW Golf, kitted out in full riding gear. Assuming that she's been to the pony club, the Goods pop round for a cuppa and ask Margo if they can go to the club to see whether there's any spare manure going. Margo says they can't because they'll offend the members, frighten the horses and lower the tone, announcing that if they set foot in the club she'll never speak to them again!

But, as Tom points out to Barbara, Margo doesn't own the place, so they go along anyway. Meeting the owner, Mrs Holman, they share a joke with her about the size of Mrs Dooms-Patterson's mount before being invited to help themselves to manure. At the same time they discover that Margo, who claims to go riding twice a week, has not in fact done so for two months. When Jerry mentions later that Margo comes home from riding exhausted, the Goods suspect she's having an affair. Their fears deepen when they spot her furtively entering an unmarked green door in the high street.

When Jerry tells Tom and Barbara that he's decided to share his wife's hobby and join the pony club himself, they try hard to dissuade him, knowing that he won't find Margo there! But his mind is made up and he heads off to see Mrs Holman. Meanwhile, Tom and Barbara confront Margo, asking why she's deceiving her husband. Appearing unperturbed, she accuses them of nosiness, and when they warn her that Jerry is on his way to join the riding club, they can't believe how cool she remains.

Tom and Barbara work themselves up into a frenzy worrying about the situation. When Jerry arrives home and everything remains peaceful next door, they become even more highly strung, as Margo and Jerry notice when they pop round to ask their friends out for a drink. As it turns out, Jerry never made it to the pony club and so never discovered Margo's secret – that she had been covertly going to Weight Watchers!

3: Our Speaker Today…

Original transmission: Sunday, 24 April 1977, BBC1, 8.20pm

First repeat: Thursday, 16 November 1978, BBC1, 8.00pm

Original viewing figures: 14.1 million

ADDITIONAL CAST FOR THIS EPISODE

Lady Truscott . . . . Angela Thorne

Bus conductor . . . . Con Chambers

Mr Batty . . . . Colin McCormack

Lad . . . . Robert Lindsay

When Mrs Wormwood, the local librarian, contracts laryngitis and is unable give her planned talk to the Townswomen's Guild, Margo asks Barbara to step in and discuss the virtues of self-sufficiency. Barbara isn't keen on the idea, but when she sees how much it means to Margo – particularly as Lady Truscott is the guest of honour – she reluctantly agrees to give a 20-minute talk.

Panic sets in the moment Margo leaves, but the talk is a huge success and the next day Margo's phone is red-hot with people ringing to compliment Barbara's performance. When Lady Truscott calls, asking Margo to congratulate Barbara and to arrange a meeting with her, Jerry is ordered to fetch a hamper from Fortnum & Mason's and drag Mrs Pearson away from her bingo to clean the house. As far as Margo is concerned, Tom and Barbara's house is *not* a fit place in which to entertain a local dignitary, so she plans to hold the meeting at her own home. The trouble is, before she can let anyone know, Lady Truscott arrives and heads for the Goods'. There are no airs and graces about Lady Truscott (who likes to be called George) as she chats to Tom over a pea-pod burgundy. Lady Truscott asks Barbara if she'll give a talk to her branch of the National Association for the Deaf, which Barbara finds hard to refuse.

Barbara's talks are so successful that she's soon being booked by all the local charities, leaving Tom to do all the work in the garden. It's something she feels guilty about, especially when she returns from one session to find the animals roaming loose and Tom nowhere to be seen. It turns out that Lenin, the cockerel, has escaped and jumped onto a No. 71 bus destined for Kingston. And it's a long walk back!

Realizing that her presence is badly needed at home, Barbara makes the decision to retire from her role as a public speaker, but not before agreeing to perform her swan-song at Grant House. However, when Tom discovers that the venue is a remand home, he decides to go along as well. The talk is an outstanding success, but for all the wrong reasons.

When Tom asks one of the young lads whether the audience were so spellbound because they're keen on the subject of self-sufficiency, he discovers the real reason for Barbara's warm reception – the fact that she was wearing a see-through dress!

4: The Weaver's Tale

Original transmission: Sunday, 1 May 1977, BBC1, 8.05pm
First repeat: Thursday, 23 November 1978, BBC1, 8.00pm
Original viewing figures: 14.6 million

ADDITIONAL CAST FOR THIS EPISODE

Ernie . . . . Milton Johns

After selling their soft fruit, the Goods find themselves left with a £10 float once all the year's bills have been accounted for. This is more spare cash than they've had for some time, and they're pleased with themselves. But their new-found wealth is short-lived when Tom, on a shopping trip to Dorking with Margo, spots a loom in a second-hand shop.

When Barbara discovers that Tom has spent all their money, she's annoyed that he didn't consult her before-hand, but they soon kiss and make up. However, she still feels his purchase was wasteful. After all, they

haven't got any wool – or a spinning wheel. When Tom states that Margo is buying them one, Barbara confesses that she may have just ruined his plan when chatting with Jerry, who feels like a slot machine 'automatically producing the jackpot' for Margo to spend. Barbara has persuaded him to put his foot down and take control of the purse-strings for once in order to change Margo's spendthrift habits.

Later that evening Margo bursts into Tom and Barbara's house after arguing with Jerry, and wants to move in. But their tiff is soon resolved. Jerry brings round a peace offering the next day, in the form of a spinning wheel. He admits he misses his wife around the house, but his change of heart is also partly due to the fact that he has to entertain some Poles shortly and hasn't a clue what they eat. The smile that spreads across Tom's face at the sight of the spinning wheel soon vanishes when it turns out to be a musical one!

THE WRITERS' CHOICE

FAVOURITE EPISODE

Bob Larbey's favourite episode of *The Good Life* comes from the third series. 'I like "The Windbreak War",' he says. 'They all got drunk in that episode, on Tom's pea-pod wine, probably. All the cast wanted to get drunk in one of the episodes, so John and I said, "Bugger it, let's have them all drunk together and get it over with." The show was a good mix of quiet moments and funny moments, which sums up a lot about its quality, I feel.'

Coincidentally, 'The Windbreak War' turns out to be John Esmonde's favourite episode, too. 'The actors were great, because they all got drunk in different ways. When people play drunk, often it's a sort of template performance, but that's not the case in this episode. Despite their different approaches, they were interlocking really well in their drunkenness and were all very good at it.'

LEAST FAVOURITE EPISODE

Surprisingly, Bob Larbey's least favourite episode was 'Anniversary'. 'It was a very sad episode, where Tom and Barbara's house gets burgled. You could hear the audience reaction when we revealed the set, and there were tears all round because everyone was so upset. It was well written and beautifully played, but it went slightly over the edge and got too sad. People couldn't stand the Goods being burgled, partly because they had so little in the first place. With nothing to steal, the criminals had vandalized the place and messed everything up. For me, it didn't altogether work, although it was still a good episode.'

As far as John Esmonde is concerned, 'Pig's Lib', from the first series, was the worst episode. 'I wasn't very happy with that one, because many of the scenes were a bit adolescent. There were a couple of scenes that could have been better written, but when you've got so many to write, it's only to be expected, I suppose.'

5: Suit Yourself

Original transmission: Sunday, 8 May 1977, BBC1, 7.15pm

First repeat: Thursday, 30 November 1978, BBC1, 8.00pm

Original viewing figures: 12.5 million

ADDITIONAL CAST FOR THIS EPISODE

Sir	Reginald Marsh
Snetterton	Philip Madoc
Dalby	Terence Conoley
Mrs Dalby	Patricia Driscoll

Margo and Jerry come across Tom on the golf course, but he hasn't taken up the sport, he's just 'raping Mother Nature' by collecting nettles. Back home, the Leadbetters see Barbara arrive on the Goods' motorized vehicle with a pile of sheep's fleeces – payment from Mr Greaves in return for a couple of days' hard labour on his sheep farm.

Margo is so curious as to why they need nettles and fleeces that she pops next door, where she finds Barbara and Tom dyeing wool for cloth-making. Margo is intrigued, so Tom gives her a conducted tour of their cottage industry, including a loom demonstration. She can't believe it when they tell her they're planning to make their own clothes.

Jerry arrives home from work and announces that 'the balloon's gone up'. He and Margo have been invited by the boss to the Fatted Calf, so he must be about to announce his retirement from JJM Ltd. Desperate to replace 'Sir' as managing director, Jerry admits that it's not a one-man race: Snetterton and Dalby have been invited, too. Jerry and Margo are faced with the challenge of outclassing the competition and one of the first things to sort out is what they're going to wear. One thing Jerry's sure about is that it won't be any of Tom's home-made efforts, even though Tom's planning to make a suit for himself!

Before setting off for the Fatted Calf, Jerry and Margo pop into the Goods' house, dressed up to the nines in their quest to creep their way into the MD's chair. At the pub everyone laughs at Sir's jokes and fawns throughout the entire evening, until he finally announces that he'll be retiring at the end of the month. Dalby attempts a toast, which Snetterton finishes for

him, but Margo and Jerry get in on the act, too. Sir announces that his successor will be one of the faces around the table, and he gets Snetterton, Dalby and Jerry to each explain why they're right for the job.

In preparation for this moment, Jerry has drawn up detailed plans explaining how he would expand the company. He panics on discovering that he's mislaid them and leaves the table, believing his hopes of promotion have been dashed. But Tom and Barbara save the day when they arrive at the pub with the missing plans. Before they leave, the Goods are spotted by Sir, who invites them over to his table. Tom takes off his coat to reveal a garish, lime-green home-made woollen suit – a real sight for sore eyes!

6: Sweet and Sour Charity

Original transmission: Sunday, 15 May 1977, BBC1, 8.05pm

First repeat: Thursday, 7 December 1978, BBC1, 8.00pm

Original viewing figures: 15 million

Jerry is in the thick of the race for promotion, now that Sir's impending retirement is official. When Tom and Barbara find him home from work early again, he tells them there's a reason. Snetterton, his main rival, is doing lots of overtime to impress the boss, so Jerry is trying a little reverse psychology. He's determined to show that he doesn't need extra hours to do a good job.

While they're enjoying a coffee, Margo arrives home from a music society meeting, annoyed that she's been outvoted by 68 to 1 over the society's next production. It seems that everyone except her wants to do *Sweet Charity*, which Margo considers 'vulgar, debased and thoroughly nasty'. To make matters worse, they want *her* to play the title role!

The next day, Tom tells Barbara that she could play Charity, because she's certainly got the wiggle. He then notices that Mrs Weaver (who has moved to Esher) has left gallons of oil in her garden tank. This sparks off an idea: Mr Greaves, a farmer they know, uses oil-fired central heating for his calves and would happily swap bales of straw for the oil. Barbara thinks taking it would be a bad idea because it amounts to stealing, but Tom feels 'acquiring' is a better word.

The matter is still playing on Tom's mind the following day, and he's furious when he finds that someone else appears to be pinching it, because it's disappearing rapidly. There's nothing else for it, he'll have to help himself to the rest. Barbara has come round to her husband's way of thinking, as the straw would be very useful, but she persuades him to call Mrs Weaver first to ask her permission. They use the Leadbetters' phone, and after Mrs Weaver has told them they're welcome to the oil, they rush back to their garden to syphon it off. But the tank is already empty, and to make matters worse, it's because the oil has leaked into their garden, ruining the soil. Barbara suddenly experiences a sinking feeling!

7: Anniversary

Original transmission: Sunday, 12 May 1977, BBC1, 8.05pm
First repeat: Thursday, 14 December 1978, BBC1, 8.00pm
Original viewing figures: 12 million

ADDITIONAL CAST FOR THIS EPISODE
Sir . . . . Reginald Marsh

As Tom remarks, the Goods' back garden looks like 'Texas gone wrong', thanks to the leaking oil tank. A large proportion of it will be out of action for years, and polluted soil bodes ill for cultivating crops. To compound the problem, Geraldine the goat has gone on strike and stopped producing milk. If no growing space in the garden is to be lost, there's only one solution – to move the pigsty to the area contaminated with oil. But money will have to be found to pay for the concrete floor they'll need.

With cashflow a perennial headache, Barbara gets out their old LPs, and, although many have sentimental value, she and Tom cart them round to Margo to see if she'll sell them to her music society chums. Barging in through the French windows, they set off Margo's new burglar alarm, which she's just had installed as a precaution against the spate of burglaries that have been taking place in the vicinity. This increase in local crime doesn't worry Tom. He can't imagine anyone bothering with their house, as there's nothing in it worth stealing.

Next day, preparing to celebrate Tom's 42nd birthday, Barbara has made an extra fairy cake to commemorate the second anniversary of their becoming self-sufficient. Tom is a little depressed because things haven't been going too well recently, but Barbara soon lifts his gloom by enthusing over the last two years being the happiest of her life.

Since the Leadbetters are also feeling down, because Jerry's chances of getting the managing director's job are looking slim, the Goods decide to ask them round for cakes and champagne (so long as Jerry brings the bubbly). They go next door to issue the invitation, only to find that Jerry and Margo have a visitor – Sir, who's come to tell Jerry he has got the job after all. When Sir heads off to enjoy his retirement, everyone is so excited that they return to the Goods' house to celebrate. They can't believe their eyes on discovering that the lounge has been vandalized. The villains have even ripped up Tom's birthday card.

Feeling sorry for his neighbours, Jerry offers Tom his old job back, if only until they're back on their feet again. But Barbara's positive attitude shines through and she cheers Tom up by convincing him that they can rise above their problems and soldier on. It's time to toast the good life!

CHRISTMAS
SPECIAL

Silly, but it's Fun

Original transmission: Monday, 26 December 1977, BBC1, 7.35pm
First repeat: Thursday, 1 January 1981, BBC1, 7.55pm
Original viewing figures: 17 million

ADDITIONAL CAST FOR THIS EPISODE
Bill . . . . David Battley

The festive spirit is in abundance at the Goods' house, with paper chains even adorning the pigsty. Meanwhile next door, Christmas is cancelled! Having specifically ordered a nine-foot tree, Margo finds, when it's delivered, that it measures a few inches short. Characteristically, she feels this is indicative of the 'depths to which standards have fallen'. Deciding to make a stand, she sends the tree back together with all the other goodies she'd ordered for Christmas. What she hadn't anticipated was that the shop would be unable to re-deliver in time for the big day.

Margo spends Christmas morning on the phone cancelling all her arrangements, pretending that Jerry has chickenpox. To Jerry it all seems a blessing in disguise, as Christmas for him is normally an endless round of socializing with the bores from Margo's pony club and music society. However, when he realizes they don't have any food or drink in the house, things don't look quite so rosy.

For the Goods, Christmas doesn't come in a van, and all it's cost them is 15p. They feel sorry for their neighbours and invite them round to their place. Tom and

Barbara's idea of a gentle, relaxing Christmas is warmly received, as are the home-made crackers – except that Margo struggles to understand the joke in hers, while everyone else is rolling around the sofa in hysterics.

The afternoon is spent playing party games, Margo's suggestion of bridge or canasta having been firmly rejected. When she finds it hard to let her hair down and be 'silly' like the others, Tom decides it's time to have a quiet word. He escorts her to the kitchen and warns her that if she doesn't start enjoying herself soon, she'll be sent home. Margo explains to Tom that it's not that she doesn't want to join in, it's just that she doesn't know how.

But she makes an effort, helped along by several glasses of Tom's pea-pod burgundy, and before long is hiccuping and claiming it's the best Christmas she's ever had. Before the evening ends it's time to exchange presents, and while the Leadbetters receive jumbo-sized home-made jumpers (that will never see the light of day), the Goods are delighted to be given a cow!

ROYAL COMMAND PERFORMANCE

A special performance of the programme, recorded in the presence of Her Majesty The Queen and His Royal Highness The Duke of Edinburgh

When I'm 65

Original transmission: Saturday, 10 June 1978, BBC1, 7.40pm (duration 45 minutes)

First repeat: Thursday, 26 October 1978, BBC1, 8.00pm (duration 30 minutes)

Original viewing figures: 14.4 million

ADDITIONAL CAST FOR THIS EPISODE

Mr Downs . . . . George Cole
Taxi driver . . . . Steve Ismay

Jerry is undergoing a medical because he's taking out a new retirement annuity (even though he's got thirteen policies already). It's the Leadbetters' way of preparing for retirement, as they intend to continue living in style. When the doctor tells Jerry he's been abusing his body

and has only just scraped through the medical, he vows to do something about it.

Meanwhile, the reality of what lies ahead for the Goods hits home as Barbara bemoans the fact that they've been unable to put anything away as a nest egg for their retirement. When they're old and unable to work any more, they'll be penniless, with no occupational pension to see them through. Tom becomes depressed and contemplates how quickly time passes, asking rhetorically: 'Whatever happened to the nit lady, clothing coupons and proper footballs with laces that cut your forehead open when you headed them?'

The next day Barbara and Tom (who by now has perked up a bit) spot the Leadbetters out jogging in their tracksuits and are anxious to find out what's brought on this new craze. The doctor's advice has hit Jerry hard, so he's trying to improve his fitness.

In an attempt to make provision for his and Barbara's old age, Tom pays a visit to the bank and presents an unrealistic proposition to the manager, Mr Downs. In exchange for £2,000 a year, Tom will leave the bank his house when he dies. The manager is unimpressed with Tom's farcical scheme and accuses him of 'infantile thinking'.

Later, when Jerry asks to borrow a spanner from Tom because he wants to fix up his wall bars, Tom laughs. Jerry, believing he's now fitter, challenges his neighbour to a run. They both set off down The Avenue like Olympic sprinters, but begin flagging as they cross the common. When they almost collapse outside a pub, they call it quits and pop in for a pint. After recharging their batteries, they sprint back up The Avenue, determined not to let their wives know what they've been up to. But when a cab driver pulls up and informs them – in front of Margo and Barbara – that they left a wallet behind, accusations of cheating fill the air!

THE LOCATION TRAIL

All 30 instalments of *The Good Life* centred around the homes of Tom and Barbara Good and their neighbours, the Leadbetters. Entrusted with finding suitable properties to represent the two couples' houses for all outside filming was production manager Brian Jones, who acted as producer John Howard Davies' right-hand man throughout the show's life. Finding the right location isn't easy at the best of times, but Brian's job was made even more difficult by one of the gardens having to be churned up!

Before jumping into his car to scour the suburbs of London, Brian (now retired from the BBC) talked to the show's writers, John Esmonde and Bob Larbey. 'While John Howard Davies was concentrating on casting, I'd take a copy of the script and start thinking about locations. I found out from the writers what they had in mind for the houses and what they thought they should look like. In this case we were searching for two houses next door to each other, one loking a little more posh than the other. The ones I eventually found worked well together and matched our requirements, although the Leadbetters' home looked a little sterile – something we were able to rectify by dotting flowers, some of them plastic, around the place.'

While the producer continued the task of booking artists and bringing other departments into the fray, Brian started scouting around for the ideal spot in which to film the sitcom, a job that can take several weeks. 'But I was lucky with *The Good Life* and found the ideal houses within two weeks,' Brian recalls. Although the show was set in Surbiton, Brian looked elsewhere for logistical reasons. 'It had to be set somewhere in suburbia, that was clear from the scripts, but because Television Centre and Ealing, where the film units were based, were on the west side of London, I needed somewhere that was easy to get to. No overnight stays in hotels were budgeted for, so the location had to be as convenient as possible for everybody, including the actors.'

With his A–Z of London to hand, Brian set off, travelling west along the A40, and immediately knew he was heading in the right direction. 'I was going against all the traffic coming into London, so thinking about moving artists from Television Centre and the camera unit setting off from Ealing, everyone would be travelling west, avoiding the rush-hour traffic heading in the other direction. And in the evening, when we'd finished filming, we'd be London bound whereas most of the rush-hour traffic would be heading out of the centre.'

Brian reached the small Buckinghamshire village of Stoke Poges, from where he began moving backwards and forwards, north and south, until he arrived at Rickmansworth and Northwood. He recalls, 'All I was doing was looking at roads and houses, and one day I turned a corner, drove down Kewferry Road, and thought, "Yes, this is it." It was as simple as that.'

Easy to reach via the A40 and set in a quiet corner of suburbia, Kewferry Road in Northwood seemed the ideal location, and two houses that Brian had photographed fitted the bill perfectly. After showing the snaps to John Howard Davies and getting the green light, the next stage in securing the houses for location work was to approach the owners.

TOM & BARBARA'S HOUSE

You might think that finding owners willing to let the BBC rip up their gardens and have pigs and chickens running all over the place would be nigh-on impossible, but not so. Michael and Margaret Mullins, who owned the house used by the Goods, didn't mind a bit. 'We'd been living there about two years,' says Margaret, 'and hadn't done anything much to the garden. It really needed digging up and starting again, so we were quite happy when the BBC told us of their intentions.'

It was a dull November day when John Howard Davies and Brian Jones knocked on the Mullins' front door to ask their permission to film in the garden, a morning Margaret remembers vividly. 'It was such an unexpected visit that I asked to see their identification,' she says. 'They wanted a quick decision, but I told them they'd have to speak to my husband that evening.'

Michael Mullins was pleased to give his consent. 'My initial thought was that it was my wife's problem rather than mine. Being at home during the day, she'd be the one who had to put up with all the upheaval. As far as I was concerned, it sounded fun.'

Production Manager Brian Jones found the Mullins 'amenable and friendly' as he explained the idea behind the BBC's new sitcom, making sure he used Richard Briers' name as the hook. 'I dropped Dickie's name an awful lot – he should get royalties,' laughs Brian, 'because that was the carrot I dangled in front of everybody. I'd tell them it was a new series with Richard Briers about self-sufficiency, and everyone said, "Oh, Richard Briers!"'

Brian surveyed the front and back gardens and found they were the ideal length for carrying out filming. 'The back garden seemed to go on forever,' he says. 'Then I had to break the news that we wanted to turn it into a smallholding, with a chicken coop, pigs and a goat, and vegetables planted every-where else.' There was silence, and Brian thought he'd blown the negotiations. 'I thought, "Here we go, I've killed it now."' However, on the proviso that the garden was restored to some form of order afterwards, the Mullins were happy, although at times they must have wondered whether normality would ever return. Michael got used to coming home from work to find water being sprayed over the house roof to represent rain, the garden turned into a quagmire, and animals being herded to and fro.

Having the garden turned into a mud-pit was one of the requirements for 'Backs to the Wall', the final episode in the first series. When a storm causes havoc with the Goods' harvest, it's imperative for the crop to be brought in. With the help of Margo and Jerry,

who's in plaster after breaking a leg while on holiday in Kenya, they set about rescuing their produce from the mud. Margo, keen to show how useful she can be, swings a sack of spuds over her shoulder and in the process accidentally knocks Barbara over, who in turn brings Jerry and Tom down into the mud with her.

It was a classic scene that Brian Jones remembers well. 'This scene needed one take, you couldn't do it in two – or so we thought. We rehearsed and rehearsed and finally decided to record. The cameraman was ready and everybody knew what was expected, so we started filming. When the scene was completed, John turned to the cameraman and said, "Well?" He paused before replying, "I'd like to go again, please." Felicity, Paul and Richard were still lying in the mud, when he added "I'm not sure, but I might have moved the camera and lost part of the action." So the next half-hour was taken up with cleaning all the mud off the actors and drying their clothes. Although we shot a second time, it turned out that the original filming was fine after all. But it made for a wonderful scene.'

What no one had anticipated, especially Michael and Margaret Mullins, was that a further three series would be commissioned, involving yet more filming at Kewferry Road. 'It dragged on a bit,' admits Michael, 'but I don't think anyone in the street had any complaints, they were all keen to come along and see what was happening.'

'I think the neighbours, on the whole, enjoyed it,' says Margaret. 'They used to come and watch, and I always made sure, before it started, that I told every-one what was going to happen. No one seemed to find it a problem. But the programme was a success, which helped, and everyone in the production team was very pleasant to us and the neighbours.'

One neighbour was Barbara Appleton, who still lives in Kewferry Road. 'No one had any real prob-lems with the filming, we were all rather intrigued.' Barbara enjoyed watching the creation of the sub-urban sitcom so much that she longed to be an extra in one of the episodes. 'In those days I walked to Northwood to do the shopping, and when I got to where they were filming I'd linger a bit, hoping they'd see me and ask whether I'd like to be involved – but that never happened,' she smiles.

Like most people affected by the filming, Barbara wondered whether their peaceful, leafy road would ever be the same again, thanks to the sitcom, which was being transmitted around the globe. 'I've often pointed out the houses to people,' admits Barbara, 'and when you tell people you live near the houses where *The Good Life* was filmed, they're always interested. One of my sons lives in Nairobi, and all his Kenyan friends have seen it and are interested in the fact that we live here.'

The Mullins – who left Kewferry Road just after the final series finished – were aware of the interest the sitcom created, but it didn't bother them too much. 'There was a period when we noticed people driving by and peering in, but as we lived in the back of the house, we didn't take much notice.'

Overall, they enjoyed the experience of loaning their home to the BBC, but they were disappointed not to receive an invitation to the Royal Command Performance. 'We'd moved down the road by the time that particular episode came along,' explains Margaret, 'and didn't receive an invite. That was a bit hurtful, especially as we'd been so involved with the show for so long. But on the whole it was good fun.'

MARGO & JERRY'S HOUSE

Albert Carr, the owner of the Leadbetters' house when the series began, still remembers the day the BBC came calling. 'If I get annoyed with the BBC, I phone up and give them a telling off,' he boasts. 'I remember watching a political programme one evening and feeling the interviewer was going on at his guest too much. I phoned the BBC and said I hoped the presenter would be more humble when he interviewed people in future. I was asked for my name but declined. I told them I wouldn't want to be on their programme because I liked having the last word, but they always had that!'

The next evening John Howard Davies knocked on Albert's door. 'When he introduced himself as being from the BBC, instinctively my mind went back twenty-four hours, and I said, "Oh yes, well, come in. I'm in a hurry but we can talk for a few moments."' Albert then discovered that his visitor didn't want to discuss his phone call at all, but was hoping to use his house for a new sitcom. 'All I was concerned about was how much I was going to get out of it,' he admits with a grin, 'not that it turned out to be much.' Rather than commit himself then and there, Albert said that he'd give the matter some thought. 'I said I'd take advice, but I never did. It was just a way of putting him off for a while to make sure I got as much money as possible!'

Albert Carr and his wife sold up shortly after the first series was transmitted, and John and Betty Tindall, who have since retired to Scotland, were living there when the BBC returned to film the following series. When the Tindalls viewed the house prior to making an offer, they knew it was no ordinary property. 'While we were there the BBC were putting up a trellis and other props in order to finish the series,' says John, 'so we knew there was something unusual about the place.'

But the small matter of the BBC filming in the street did not influence the Tindalls' decision to buy. 'All we thought was that we'd found a nice house, just what we were looking for. In fact, we thought the series had been simply a one-off,' admits John, who was surprised when Brian Jones returned a few months later asking to film there again. 'I felt there was some trepidation in the neighbourhood that the BBC were going to take over completely and upset what was normally a quiet and unassuming residential district. It was the sort of area where nothing ever happened – ideal for living in.' Just like the first time, however, everyone's concerns were quickly dispelled. 'Nothing serious happened to cause any real disruption – except when the restaurant car caught fire, which was potentially quite dangerous at the time!'

Brian Jones also remembers the chip-pan fire. 'It overheated, although it was sorted out when Betty Tindall called the fire brigade, who sprayed inside the van with foam – half an hour before everyone was due to break for lunch!' Filming continued while the caterer salvaged what food he could in order to come up with some fresh meals. 'He did a good job during a very testing time, and no one, as far as I remember, went without lunch.'

Although Kewferry Road was used priniciplly for outdoor shots, the interior of the Leadbetters' house, shot in the studio, was also modelled loosely on the Tindall's home. Photographs were taken inside the house looking out onto the back garden and this enabled the design team to create a realistic background for the studio set. 'When you looked through the French windows on the set, it was as if you were looking out from the house itself,' comments John Tindall.

When filming began on series two, the Tindalls were somewhat reserved about it at first. 'We were moving into an area of which we had no previous knowledge whatsoever,' admits Betty. 'But when the press began giving the show tremendous write-ups and it was referred to as being a programme with some merit, we felt that we ought to support it.'

Most of the filming took place next door, but there were times when the Tindalls' garden was used. 'There was night and day filming, but it wasn't a terrible inconvenience at all,' remarks John. 'They dug a few holes and even knocked a fence down on one occasion, but it was all repaired properly, so I had no complaints. We enjoyed watching the filming, and admired the professionalism of the actors and the production team.'

The thoughtfulness and understanding shown by Brian Jones was particularly appreciated. 'He was a very soothing person, which was valuable to us,' admits John. 'I remember coming home one Friday night to find I couldn't get my car anywhere near my own house for what seemed like a million people watching the filming. I had to walk up the road and struggle across the forecourt in front of all these people, complete with shopping. I was angry, to say the least. But Brian Jones was quick to calm me down and make me feel better. His professionalism is something I'll always remember.'

Over the years, Brian got to know the Tindalls quite well. 'John called me a con man, once,' he laughs. 'While we were renegotiating for one of the later series, he said, "You know, Brian, you're a bit of a con man, aren't you?" I was surprised at being accused of such a thing and asked what he meant. "Well, you have to persuade people, perhaps against their better judgement, to let a film unit trample all over their garden." I replied, "Yes, I suppose I do. I've never thought about it in that way." I told him that I always approach things as honestly as possible, telling everyone as much as I can, because I wouldn't want

any surprises myself under those circumstances. John then turned to me and asked whether I'd allow a film unit into my own garden, to which I replied, "No way. I know some of them aren't as nice as we are!"'

The Tindalls were impressed with how smoothly everything went. 'All of the technical staff showed a professionalism that took my breath away,' says John. 'Everyone knew their job and worked with precision, especially when it came to the studio recording. I think our house was involved in about twenty-three episodes, and we were given invitations to see every one of them being recorded at the studio. As well as being invited into the audience, we were allowed to go into the director's gallery and the sound gallery.'

The juxtaposition of the Leadbetters' and the Goods' houses was helped by introducing colour, in the form of some artificial flowers and such items as a wheelbarrow packed with plastic blooms. This caused a certain amount of interest locally, as Betty Tindall recalls. 'I remember this woman walking her dog and noticing the wheelbarrow. She said, "Isn't it amazing what some people will do just to make their garden look pretty." The woman obviously thought it was our idea. But it certainly looked effective on the TV.'

Brian Jones agrees with Betty. 'You can't tell the difference on screen, not unless you get very close to the flowers,' he says. 'Anyway, viewers aren't interested in the flowers, they're watching the actors. If they end up looking too closely at the dressing of the set, no matter how good and accurate it is, there's something wrong with the dialogue, the actors or some other aspect of the production.'

Filming for each of the four series usually took about two weeks, during which the residents got to know the production team well. But the Tindalls weren't sad when the sitcom finally reached an end. 'We were glad it was all over, to be honest,' says John. 'We weren't star-struck or anything. We just wanted to get on with our lives, glad that something we'd undertaken had been successfully completed. However, we were pleased that the little we'd done had contributed to an enormously successful series.'

If the same situation arose again, and the Tindalls were asked to allow filming on their property, they wouldn't be so quick to accept. 'If we were offered the same terms and conditions, we'd say, "No, thank you." In fact, if we'd owned the house from the very beginning of the series, we'd have probably refused. But the show was up and running when they asked us, so we felt it was the decent thing to do.'

At the time, there was speculation about how much the owners of the two houses in Kewferry Road were being paid for allowing the BBC to film there. In fact, they were paid in the region of £50 an episode – certainly not the sort of amounts being bandied about. 'Newspaper reports said people were paying off their mortgages from the proceeds,' says Betty, 'but that was far from the truth. It might have taken us and a couple of friends out for a meal, but that was about it.'

On the strength of newspaper reports inflating the disturbance fees, the Tindalls found themselves being questioned by the Inland Revenue, as John explains. 'The taxman showed an unusual interest in my income for about three years, presumably suspecting that all the newspaper reports must be right, despite the fact that I'd sent him copies of all my correspondence with the BBC.'

Now, twenty-five years after the first series was screened, John and Betty enjoy watching repeats. 'It's great seeing our old house again, and whenever an episode is shown, friends are always intrigued, knowing that our house was used. It was an interesting experience.'

COMING BACK FOR MORE...

By the time John Esmonde and Bob Larbey were commissioned to write a second series, the locations in Northwood had become an integral part of the show. It was unthinkable that substitute houses could be found for the two in Kewferry Road. Brian Jones had to be a great diplomat in order to keep everyone happy and on his side. His tact and diplomacy, mixed with honesty and openness, were qualities that gave him a sound footing when it came to conducting negotiations and arranging matters with the residents. Nevertheless, at times it would have been useful to be a magician!

'I certainly had to keep a lot of balls in the air at the same time,' he comments. 'I made sure I did my homework thoroughly, so that I could nip any problems in the bud.'

In all the time he worked on the show, Brian can only recall a couple of instances when he received complaints from people living nearby, and on both occasions the matter was resolved quickly. 'They were negligible, nothing really to worry about. There was one guy who got a bit twitchy when some of the crew parked their cars too close to his drive. And another man, who lived near Kewferry Road, got a bit grouchy and told me he didn't like us being there. I remember saying to him, "I'm sorry if we were disturbing you, we won't be long." He complained, "This is the third time you've been back." I knew that we'd probably be back for a fourth time, but I didn't feel it would be wise to tell him that! As far as he was concerned, the sooner we left the better.'

Brian doesn't blame people for being grumpy, and can sympathize with them. 'There are an awful lot of people, perhaps as many as thirty, involved in recording a show like *The Good Life*. You always think you should be able to reduce the number, but you can't, because the cameraman can't do the sound man's job, the make-up people can't do the costume department's job, and so on. They're very specific kinds of profession, and although they all work together you can't substitute any of them. It's just not practical.'

Fortunately, problems were few and far between. 'Everything worked well. I tend to go by the principle that if something works, don't fix it. I never had any complaints from the writers, or the producer, so everyone must have been happy,' says Brian, to whom Kewferry Road must have felt like a second home. Including outdoor shots for the Royal Command Performance, the BBC filmed there on five separate occasions. 'Because of the logistics of production and the transmission schedules, we couldn't simply record the four series and the Command Performance one after the other. It was spread over several years.'

One series had to be recorded earlier in the year than normal, even though the scripts were set in the summertime. This created a few headaches, as Brian explains. 'Every outdoor scene had to be shot tight so that you couldn't tell there weren't any leaves on the trees. It was so cold, you could see the actors' breath. And, of course, Penelope and Felicity had to wear lightweight clothes because it was supposed to be summer. Such happy memories!'

JOHN HOWARD DAVIES

THE PRODUCER

John Howard Davies entered the film industry as a child actor and starred in many pictures during the late 1940s and early '50s, most notably David Lean's 1948 production of *Oliver Twist* (as Oliver, at the age of nine), *The Rocking Horse Winner* (1950), *The Magic Box* (1951) and *Tom Brown's Schooldays*, in which he again played the lead.

Son of the writer Jack Davies, John was brought up in London and attended Haileybury School and Imperial Services College, giving up film work to concentrate on completing his education.

After carrying out his national service in the Royal Navy, he began his adult working life as a clerk in a City finance company, earning £7 a week, and later spent six months as a trainee carpet salesman in a Bournemouth department store. Unsure where his future lay, John gave in his notice and decided to travel the world. He drove a bus to India and hitch-hiked to Australia, where he returned to the stage, appearing at the Australian National Theatre in several productions, including *The Sound of Music*.

As roles became ever harder to find, he gave up the idea of trying to make it as an adult actor and returned to England. After a brief spell selling lubricating oil in Wembley, in 1967 John joined the BBC as a production assistant. Two years later he was promoted to producer, his early credits including *The World of Beachcomber*, *All Gas and Gaiters*, *Misleading Cases*, *Steptoe and Son* and early editions of *Monty Python's Flying Circus*.

He went on to produce and direct *The Good Life*, *The Goodies*, *Fawlty Towers* and the first episode of *The Fall and Rise of Reginald Perrin*, as well as the *Blackadder* pilot. During this period he earned BAFTA awards for his work on both *Monty Python* and *Fawlty Towers*.

John was promoted to Head of Comedy at the BBC in 1978, and in the five years for which he headed that department he was responsible for commissioning many of the Corporation's classic shows: *Yes, Minister*, *Not the Nine o'Clock News*, *To the Manor Born*, *Butterflies*, *Hi-De-Hi!*, *Only Fools and Horses*, *Bread*, *Just Good Friends* and *'Allo, 'Allo*.

He became the BBC's Head of Light Entertainment in 1982, but three years afterwards returned to production, this time with Thames TV, for whom he produced programmes including *Executive Stress*, starring Penelope Keith and Geoffrey Palmer. In 1988 he was appointed Controller of Light Entertainment, a job he combined with producing and directing *No Job for a Lady* and *Hope It Rains*.

He also directed the first episode of *Men Behaving Badly* and both produced and directed the first three episodes of *Mr Bean*, which won the Golden Rose, the Press Prize and the City of Montreux Comedy Prize at the Montreux Festival, as well as a BANFF and an International Emmy.

Nowadays John Howard Davies works freelance, directing commercials as well as the occasional show for TV, such as *The Vicar of Dibley* Easter Special. He lives in Oxfordshire with his daughter and son. His main leisure interest is painting and he is a member of the Welsh shooting team.

JOHN HOWARD DAVIES' TV CREDITS INCLUDE –

AS PRODUCER/DIRECTOR:

Fawlty Towers (Series 1, 1975)

We'll Think of Something (1986)

All in Good Faith (1986–7)

Andy Capp (1988)

The Labours of Erica (1989)

Mr Bean (Nos 1–3, 1990–1)

No Job for a Lady (1990–2)

A Slight Hitch (1991)

Hope It Rains (1991–2)

Law and Disorder (1994)

AS EXECUTIVE PRODUCER:

Mr Bean (No. 4, 1991)

After Henry (1992)

AS PRODUCER:

Misleading Cases (1967–8)

The World of Beachcomber (1968)

As Good Crooks Go (1969)

Monty Python's Flying Circus (Nos 1–4, 1969)

The Very Merry Widow (1969)

All Gas and Gaiters (1969–71)

The Goodies (1970–2)

It's Awfully Bad for your Eyes, Darling... (pilot, 1971)

Steptoe and Son (1972)

The Rescue (1973)

Whoops Baghdad (1973)

A Girl's Best Friend (1974)

No Strings (1974)

The Good Life (1975–8)

The Fall and Rise of Reginald Perrin (No. 1, 1976)

The Other One (1977)

Blackadder (pilot, 1983)

Executive Stress (1986–7)

Men Behaving Badly (pilot)

No Limit

AS DIRECTOR:

The Vicar of Dibley (Easter Special, 1996)

SHARING THEIR VIEWS

As far as Richard Briers was concerned, it was important having someone as experienced as John Howard Davies producing *The Good Life*. Having acted himself, he could understand and appreciate the actor's perspective.

He was very passionate about the show, believing in it wholeheartedly. I've been lucky enough to work with some very talented directors, and John was certainly one of them. He used to give us all a kind of pep talk before we recorded the show, which helped a great deal. He drew the unit together and we were very lucky to have him.

RICHARD BRIERS

John Esmonde and Bob Larbey also considered themselves lucky to have John Howard Davies produce their sitcom.

He was terrific. We used to love the way he'd sit very close to the actors when they rehearsed. He was sharp and good at everything he did. We kept thinking, 'My God, hasn't he done that well.' I never looked at anything he'd done without feeling admiration.

BOB LARBEY

John was sensational. When he directs, it's done in a hushed manner – there are never any raised voices. He has the ability to keep scenes flowing while continuing to put forward his comments and direction. He would always ask our opinion, because it was all about making the series as good as possible.

JOHN ESMONDE

FAMILIAR FACES

In addition to the main quartet, 53 other actors were given dialogue in *The Good Life*. While some made their living playing small character parts on TV, others were stalwarts of the sitcom genre. These are some of the people who appeared during the run of the show.

BRUCE BOULD
(b. Bradford)
Role: Guy (Series 2, episode 2)

When, as a ten-year-old, Bruce Bould starred as Toad in *Toad of Toad Hall* in a children's amateur production at Bradford Civic Playhouse, he knew he wanted to be an actor. His dreams became reality when, at the age of 17 and a year into his A-level studies, he was invited to join Birmingham Rep as acting ASM. He worked there for four months before studying at RADA, in the knowledge that there would be a job waiting for him upon graduation.

In 1969 he returned to Birmingham and completed another three years at the Rep, during which he first met his wife, actress Theresa Watson.

By the mid-1970s Bruce had already played several small parts on television, including his debut in *Z Cars*, *New Scotland Yard* and his first leading role in an episode of the BBC's *Churchill's People* in 1975. After appearing in two successful plays, *Clever Soldiers* and, for six months, *A Family and a Fortune*, he appeared in *The Good Life* – his first sitcom – as the hero-worshipping student, Guy.

Bruce, who is best known for playing the diffident David Harris-Jones in *The Fall and Rise of Reginald Perrin*, has since been seen in numerous TV shows, including *To the Manor Born*, *Shelley*, *Drop the Dead Donkey*, *Strangers*, *Shine On Harvey Moon* and three series of *Howard's Way*.

TERENCE CONOLEY
(b. Colchester)
Role: Donald Dalby (Series 4, episode 5)

On leaving school, Terence served nine years in the army before leaving the forces in search of a fresh challenge. He studied music and drama for four years, and after graduating entered the world of repertory theatre. He performed around the country, establishing his name in the acting profession. Work in films and TV soon followed. On the big screen he was seen in such films as *Tiara Tahiti*, while on television he appeared in *Misleading Cases*, *The Fall and Rise of Reginald Perrin*, *Fawlty Towers* and many other shows.

MOYRA FRASER
(b. Sydney, Australia)
Role: Felicity – the wife of 'Sir'
(Series 1, episodes 2 & 6)

Moyra moved to England when a baby of six months and by the age of twelve was a promising ballet dancer. She left school early to accept a scholarship with Sadlers Wells Ballet. After completing her training, she joined the company and had her first big success in Robert Helpmann's *Comas*.

She stayed with the company for several years before leaving to play the principal dancing and acting role in the musical *Song of Norway* at the Palace Theatre. After being offered parts in other musicals and pantomimes, she also appeared in opera and revue.

In her early thirties she began concentrating on acting, her growing list of theatre credits including spells with the English Stage Company at the Royal Court, appearances in *As You Like It*, *The Double Dealer*, *The Merry Wives of Windsor* and *Richard II*, and international tours with *On Approval* and *The Rivals*.

On television Moyra has appeared in numerous programmes – for example *Hancock*, *Danger UXB*, *Driveway*, two series of Central's *From the Top* (as Annie), *Grange Hill* and *Jeeves and Wooster*. She also played Dame Caroline Troye in *The House of Eliott*. But Moyra is probably best known for her portrayal of Penny in *As Time Goes By* with Judi Dench and Geoffrey Palmer. In addition, she has acted in several films, most notably Ken Russell's *The Boyfriend*.

ROBERT GILLESPIE
(b. Lille, France)
Role: Mr Carter (Series 1, episode 4)

Robert spent his early years in France but later moved with his parents to Manchester, performing at the city's Library Theatre on a semi-professional basis before going to RADA. After graduating he worked at the Old Vic until offered the role of Matthew in the television production of *Jesus of Nazareth*.

Although Robert is normally seen in comedy roles – such as the gas man in *Rising Damp*, a policeman in *Whatever Happened to the Likely Lads?*, five series playing Dudley Rush in *Keep It in the Family* and other parts in *Robin's Nest*, *Butterflies*, *George and Mildred* and *Dad's Army* – he has also appeared in a host of dramas, including *Maigret*, *Crane*, *New Scotland Yard*, *The Sweeney*, *Van der Valk*, *The Professionals* and *Secret Army*.

Robert, who also writes and directs, has made several films as well as doing regular stage work, including two years with the Royal Shakespeare Company.

PHILIP MADOC
(b. Merthyr Tydfil)
Role: Snetterton
(Series 4, episode 5)

After working as an interpreter in Germany, Philip entered the acting profession in the 1960s, having studied at RADA. He worked for several years in rep before moving into television, in which medium one of his first appearances was in the 1956 production *The Count of Monte Cristo*. Among his subsequent TV work have been the roles of Detective Chief Supt. Tate in *Target* and Fison in *A Very British Coup*, and others in *Dad's Army*, *The Avengers* and *Dr Who*.

Philip has also made more than 30 films, such as *The Quiller Memorandum*, *Daleks: Invasion Earth* and *Operation Daybreak*. In recent years he has worked mainly in the theatre but has also appeared in his own detective series on TV, *A Mind to Kill*, which has been shown around the world.

CHARMIAN MAY
(b. Hampshire)
Role: Mrs Weaver (Series 2, episodes 6 & 7)

Joining RADA straight from convent school, Charmian later worked for 15 years in rep, where she played many classical roles, before making her television debut in *Second Time Around*. In the course of a busy career she has acted in four series of *You're Only Young Twice* as Miss Milton, appeared in *Nanny*, *Don't Wait Up*, *The Darling Buds of May* and *The Fall and Rise of Reginald Perrin*, and played Miranda, the lady captain in *The 19th Hole* and a school secretary in *Soldier, Soldier*. She has also made several film appearances.

Charmian has directing as well acting experience, and has also written her own one-woman show, *Celebrating Shakespeare*, which she has presented in both the UK and the USA.

ANGELA THORNE
(b. Karachi, Pakistan)
Role: Lady Truscott (Series 4, episode 3)

Angela (who was four months pregnant when she appeared in *The Good Life*) moved to England as a child and by the age of twelve had decided that she wanted to be an actress. Unsure how to join the profession, she left school and completed a secretarial course, then worked for a year as a secretary at the Indonesian Embassy in London.

Chatting with a drama student at a party led to the opportunity to audition for a professor at the Guildhall School of Music and Drama, on whose advice Angela enrolled for evening classes in drama. Afterwards she won a scholarship to the

Guildhall. Lack of finance prevented her from studying beyond the first year, but luckily she stepped straight into employment, touring the country with a children's theatre before turning to rep work, initially as an ASM at a theatre in Paignton, Devon.

Her first taste of a major London production was at the Haymarket Theatre in *You Never Can Tell*, with Ralph Richardson, in the early 1960s – a break that led to numerous other West End appearances. While Angela was appearing in the play she was sent to see Ned Sherrin, who was recording a musical for the BBC, called *Take a Sapphire*. The meeting resulted in Angela making her television debut as a princess in the final scenes.

From there she went on to appear in *That Was The Week That Was*, *The Canterville Ghost* and notably *To the Manor Born*, in which sitcom her role as Marjory Frobisher made her well known to viewers. Her other TV credits include playing Maggie in *Anyone for Denis?*, Daphne Trenchard in *Three Up, Two Down* and Emma in *The Good Guys*.

Although most of Angela's career has been spent in the theatre, she enjoys working in every medium.

Other familiar faces who popped up in *The Good Life* include **TONY SELBY**, who played Sam, the rag-and-bone man who sells the Goods an old range. Born in London, Tony trained at the Italia Conti Stage Academy before entering the industry in the 1950s. A regular performer on TV, probably his best-known roles are Cpl. Marsh in Esmonde and Larbey's *Get Some In!* and Max Taplow in *Love Hurts*. Among other shows in which he has appeared are *Bergerac*, *Mulberry*, *Law and Disorder*, *The Detectives*, *The Sweeney* and *Doctor Who*. Tony has also appeared in a number of films, including *Alfie*, *Press for Time* and *Villain*. **PAMELA MANSON** appeared in the final episode of series one as Molly, one of the Goods' so-called friends. Born in London, Pamela worked as a secretary on the *News Chronicle* before becoming a professional actress in 1952. After years of theatre work, she began a TV career, concentrating on comedy. The other shows she appeared in, before her death in 1988, were *Dad's Army*, *The Professionals*, *Jackanory* and *Charles and Diana*. Mobile greengrocer Ronnie Boxall was acted by **BLAKE BUTLER**, who has also played character parts in comedy shows such as *Dad's Army*, while Lincoln-born **JOHN QUAYLE** was cast as the freelance journalist in the episode 'Mr Fix-It'. John trained at RADA before beginning a career that has taken him around the world. As well as working extensively in the theatre, on television he's played Major Willoughby-Gore in *Farrington of the FO*, Woodley in *The 19th Hole*, and roles in *Upstairs, Downstairs, Terry and June* and *Nanny*. The magistrate who sentenced Tom Good to a spell in prison was played by Beckenham-born actor **JAMES COSSINS**, who was a Silver Medal winner when at RADA. James began his career in 1951 and his extensive TV credits include *The Pickwick Papers, Some Mothers Do 'Ave 'Em*, Judge in *Citizen Smith, Fawlty Towers, Bergerac* and Meredith Bland in *Under the Hammer*. He has also made several films, such as *Scrooge, Wuthering Heights, The Lost Continent, A Fish Called Wanda, Otley, The Man with the Golden Gun, Ghandi* and *The Great Train Robbery*.

In the episode 'Our Speaker Today…' one of the lads at Grant Hall, a remand home, is played by **ROBERT LINDSAY**. Born in Ilkeston, Derbyshire, Robert trained at RADA before starting his career as an ASM in Exeter. The winner of numerous awards, he first grabbed the public's attention as Jakey Smith in *Get Some In!* and notably as Wolfie Smith in four series of *Citizen Smith*, which became something of a cult. Among Robert's many credits

are the series *Nightingales, GBH*, the film *That'll be the Day*, and *Me and My Girl* both in the West End and on Broadway. Ernie, the assistant at the second-hand shop in 'The Weaver's Tale', was played by **MILTON JOHNS**, a well-known face in TV comedy.

Milton has also been seen in *Ever Decreasing Circles, Some Mothers Do 'Ave 'Em, Butterflies, Home to Roost, Solo, Fresh Fields*, and more. His drama credits include the role of Brendan Scott in *Coronation Street* and others in *Poldark, Doctor Who* and *Trainer*. Donald Dalby's wife in 'Suit Yourself' was played by **PATRICIA DRISCOLL**, who in 1955 presented *Picture Book* as part of the BBC's classic children's programme *Watch with Mother*. Also in the 1950s, Patricia replaced Bernadette O'Farrell as Maid Marian in ABC TV's *The Adventures of Robin Hood*. **DAVID BATTLEY**, who was seen as Bill, the delivery man, in the Christmas Special of *The Good Life*, 'Silly, but it's Fun', is yet another familiar face on television. He has been in two series of *Relative Strangers* as well as acting in many other shows, such as *One Foot in the Grave, The Darling Buds of May, As Time Goes By, Lovejoy, Rutland Weekend Television* and *The Beiderbecke Affair*. And finally… the perennially popular **GEORGE COLE** made a special guest appearance in 'When I'm 65' for the Royal Command Performance of *The Good Life*, taking the part of Mr Downs, the bank manager.

SIR ALAN AYCKBOURN REMEMBERS...

Prior to the recording of the first series of Esmonde and Larbey's *The Good Life*, Alan Ayckbourn – one of Britain's most successful dramatists – had the pleasure of working with all four of its stars. Felicity Kendal was appearing in his comedy stage trilogy *The Norman Conquests* when Richard Briers asked her whether she'd like to read for the part of Barbara. So, too, was Penelope Keith, and both actresses were watched by John Howard Davies, Jimmy Gilbert and production manager Brian Jones before being offered parts in the new TV show. Meanwhile, Richard Briers was appearing in Ayckbourn's *Absent Friends* and Paul Eddington in *Absurd Person Singular*. Here, Sir Alan turns the clock back and recalls his time working with the cast.

It was a time when I was fortunate enough to have several plays running in the West End. Paul Eddington had been in *Absurd Person Singular*, Penny Keith and Felicity Kendal were doing *The Norman Conquests*, while Richard Briers was in *Absent Friends*, although he'd also appeared in a couple of my earlier shows, including *Absurd Person*. So I guess you could say I knew them all very well.

At that point I almost had my own little rep company of people who appeared in two or three of my plays. Richard, who became famous for *Marriage Lines*, first worked with me on my initial West End hit, *Relatively Speaking*, which came into London in 1967. He's a consummate actor, coming from a tradition of brilliant light comedians such as Nigel Patrick, Alastair Sim and Rex Harrison. More recently he's developed a completely different side of himself by playing, among other things, sizeable Shakespearean roles. But in those early days he was best known as a very polished young comic, with the ability and confidence to work alongside established artists like Celia Johnson and Michael Hordern.

One thing about Richard that I've always admired is his speed of delivery. He's tremendously fast, yet plays with great clarity. The art is to play fast *and* clear. Anyone can gabble, but the way he manages to combine a crispness with such speed and fast cueing is breathtaking.

Paul Eddington, meanwhile, took over from Michael Aldridge in *Absurd Person* and was probably

the least well-known of the cast when *The Good Life* started, although he rapidly made a name for himself. By the time I worked with him again in *Ten Times Table*, he was an established star in his own right. Paul was a very accomplished and skilful player, but slightly lower key than Richard, playing more off the back foot.

He stayed with *Absurd Person* for some time. I think he saw off two or three casts. There was a nice dryness to Paul that I liked very much. He preferred to undercut, as he demonstrated in *Yes, Minister,* which was right up his street. In *Ten Times Table* he played the harassed chairman of a committee that contained some strong personalities, including a fierce Marxist and an extreme right-winger. Everyone was battling for supremacy and Paul was in the midst of it all, conveying what he did best – a sort of bemused, very English, charming tolerance, all the time looking for compromise. He liked working against strong, vivid performances where he could undercut.

Actors' dressing rooms always have their own particular aura, and Paul had classical music playing in his while he read, usually some learned tome. That's how he liked spending the half-hour before he went on, gently relaxing. He was a man of great taste and civilization.

I first saw Penny Keith doing a play of mine, *How the Other Half Loves*, at Leatherhead. When I was casting *The Norman Conquests* with Eric Thompson, who directed the plays, I told him I'd seen someone who was ideal for the part of Sarah. Indeed, she turned out to be just perfect and became an overnight hit, one of the most talked-about actresses in London.

Penny – although she's nothing like it in real life – can convey, quite brilliantly, that sort of crushingly snobbish middle-class woman who's born out of great vulnerability and insecurity.

Sarah in *The Norman Conquests* was a woman who wanted everything right and proper. The famous dinner-party scene was all about 'proper' standards –

getting the seating right, for instance, even though nobody else really cared who they sat next to. But for her it was very important that they sat man, woman, man, woman. There was a life-or-death seriousness about the character, which gave the whole comic mayhem a firm core of truth.

Essentially, Sarah's dignity and sense of decorum made her the classic English farce figure, which Penelope Keith played quite beautifully. We were rather awed by her because she learnt her lines terribly fast and then appeared to be waiting around for the rest of us to catch up! She was great to work with.

As for Felicity, I remember watching her rehearse a scene with Tom Courtenay in *The Norman Conquests* and remarking to someone, 'Oh god, you just want to run over and pick her up.' She's got a very engaging personality which brings out the man in one, I always think! You really want to bound up on stage and say, 'Come on, I'll look after you.'

In the play she was Annie, a rather put-upon, downtrodden little figure, the sort of character who's slightly bullied or taken advantage of. Felicity did this wonderfully, and was terrific to have in the play.

I watched some episodes of *The Good Life* and thought it was a lovely situation comedy. It relied on truthful, unforced humour, whereas nowadays a lot of sitcoms are so jam-packed, they make you feel like you've been hit over the head. John Esmonde and Bob Larbey knew better than that. They wrote some great scripts.

All four actors were excellent performers. Some people tend to separate comedy from drama because they think each requires a different technique, but of course, the very best actors can play both. They're able to play comedy but retain the truth – the seriousness and integrity of the character. That's a great art, and one that Paul, Richard, Felicity and Penelope all mastered.

WHO'S WHO IN *THE GOOD LIFE*

Since most episodes of *The Good Life* focused on domestic settings, there was rarely any great need to employ cast members beyond the regular quartet. With all the main action taking place between the Goods and the Leadbetters in their respective homes, additional characters (other than semi-regulars like 'Sir', played by Reginald Marsh) tended to be restricted to subsidiary ones such as local shopkeepers, postmen and so on. But whether the actors who played these roles uttered a solitary line of dialogue or fifty, all played an important part in the sitcom's success. This section of the book spotlights the minor characters who were written, often briefly, into Esmonde and Larbey's scripts. Unless featured more extensively elsewhere in this book, every actor ever listed in the closing credits is mentioned, together with a brief overview of the part he or she played. The few episodes that are omitted are those that involved only the main cast members and, in some cases, 'Sir'. Also included are descriptions of some characters who, although mentioned in the scripts, are never actually seen.

SERIES ONE

1: Plough Your Own Furrow

Commissionaire (Norman Atkyns): Charles, the commissionaire at JJM Ltd, greets Jerry with a salute but can't remember Tom's name, even after eight years – much to Tom's chagrin.

Brian (Martin Neil) works for Tom at JJM as a draughtsman. He admires Tom's design for a plastic hippo to be given away inside packets of breakfast cereal, but insults him by assuming he's too old to play cricket for the department's team against Accounts.

Miss Barton (not seen in episode, just referred to by Jerry): Jerry's secretary at JJM.

2: Say Little Hen…

Felicity (Moyra Fraser) is the wife of 'Sir', who heads JJM Ltd. She is a dinner guest at the Leadbetters' on the evening Jerry wants 'Sir' to give Tom his job back. Felicity, supportive of the Goods' drive for self-sufficiency, remarks that she, too, had always wanted to do something exciting with her life – but then she married her husband.

3: The Weaker Sex?

Sam (Tony Selby), the rag-and-bone man from whom Tom buys a rusty old range, uses rhyming slang because he feels it's what customers in the snooty neighbourhood expect. But Sam is not as indigent as his job might suggest – he owns a villa in Spain and is learning the language at evening classes.

GPO Man (Paul McDowell): The character who turns up to disconnect the Goods' telephone, one of the many non-essentials discarded by Tom and Barbara in their new lifestyle.

4: Pig's Lib

Mr Carter (Robert Gillespie) is the new cravat-sporting chairman of the local residents' association, called in by Margo to resolve her dispute with the Goods over their plan to keep pigs. A reasonable kind of chap, he's in favour of Tom and Barbara's intentions, especially since he, too, broke free from a life of commuting to become a freelance writer.

ADDING A LOCAL TOUCH

Whenever possible, local residents were given the opportunity to appear as extras. In the episode 'The Thing in the Cellar' some of the local lads are seen on the riverbank, where Tom Good and Jerry Leadbetter go fishing. And in the final episode – the Royal Command Performance, 'When I'm 65' – people from the neighbourhood are seen sitting outside the pub when an exhausted Tom and Jerry stop off for a drink.

Window Cleaner (Jonathan Lynn): The man who cleans the Goods' windows and is offered home-made wine, spring onions and other produce by Barbara in payment.

Mr Wilks (Lionel Wheeler), a local shopkeeper, agrees to trade a copy of *Pig Breeder* magazine and a bag of potato peelings for eggs.

Man (John Lawrence): Known as Jack, this fellow collects the Goods'

pigs for slaughter after they stray into Margo's garden.

5: The Thing in the Cellar

Angler (Ray Mort): When Tom goes fishing with Jerry, he ends up arguing with this fellow-angler about keeping undersized fish rather than throwing them back.

6: The Pagan Rite

Waiter (John Scott Martin) serves dinner to Tom and Barbara at a posh hotel, where the Goods are staying as a much-needed treat.

7: Backs to the Wall

Doctor (June Jago): The medic who visits Tom, confirming that he's pulled muscles on both sides of his spine, which puts him out of action for seven days.

People in the pub – George, Molly, barman Ron and Harry (Billy Milton, Pamela Manson, Frank Lester and Harry Goodier): When Barbara is in desperate need of assistance to save her and Tom's harvest from ruin, she runs to the local pub and asks their 'friends' to help. But not one of them will lift a finger.

SERIES TWO

1: Just My Bill

Restaurant Owner (Wolfe Morris): Michelangelo Lombardi, proprietor of the Runcible Spoon restaurant in town, is Tom's first customer when he sells off his surplus produce, offering £70 for his home-grown vegetables.

Clerk (Frank Gatliff): Mr Squires, a clerk at the council offices, takes payment of Margo's rates.

Van Driver (Blake Butler): Ronnie Boxall, who's spent ten years building up his mobile fruit and greengrocery business and doesn't want to lose customers in The Avenue, turns nasty when Tom tries to sell off excess produce on his patch.

Woman (Ruth Kettlewell): When he spots this lady collecting for charity in the high street, Tom donates his very last penny in return for a Union Jack button.

2: The Guru of Surbiton

Guy (Bruce Bould), a 20-year-old student who boards with the Goods, helping out around the place in return for his keep, is keen to learn from his hero, Tom.

Ruth (Irene Richards), another student staying with Tom and Barbara, develops a crush for Tom but in the end leaves The Avenue to settle down with boyfriend Guy.

Mr Webster (not seen in episode, just referred to) was Tom's old barber in the days before Barbara cut his hair.

Mr & Mrs Turner (not seen in episode but referred to by Margo) are the couple who lived next door to the Goods until their house was sold to the Weavers.

3: Mr Fix-It

Mr Coles (John Quayle), a freelance journalist, writes an article about Tom and Barbara and their new lifestyle, but confusion reigns when the feature, which Margo had excitedly thought was going into *The Observer*, appears instead in a local newspaper.

Delivery Man (Steve Emerson) delivers a yacht to the Goods' house.

4: The Day Peace Broke Out

Magistrate (James Cossins): The magistrate binds Tom over for three months after an airgun incident in which he injures the man he catches stealing his leeks. The sentence is increased to 28 days' imprisonment when Tom refuses to promise that he'll keep the peace.

Harry Bennett (Brian Grellis) is the thief who helps himself to leeks from the Goods' garden. A painter and decorator by trade, to make amends he offers to paint the house for them.

6: Home, Sweet Home

Mr May (Edwin Brown) delivers a boar to the Goods' house. Coming from a family that has been farming since the 17th century, he feels that Tom and Barbara are only 'playing' at being self-sufficient and suggests they buy an eight-acre smallholding close to his own property.

Mrs Weaver (Charmian May) moves in next to the Goods and immediately gets Margo's stamp of approval – her bookshelves contain no paperbacks, she has a ceramic umbrella stand in her hallway, she's from Bournemouth and, best of all, she votes Tory. An artist by trade, Mrs Weaver paints a picture of Thames Ditton for Margo as a birthday present.

7: Going to Pot?

Mr Blundell (not seen in episode) is the tutor of the house maintenance class attended by Tom and Barbara.

Celia Fishwick (not seen in episode), Margo's friend who owns a craft studio in Chelsea, is keen to sell Tom's goblets.

SERIES THREE

2: The Happy Event

The Policeman (George Innes) is about to book the Goods for speeding – until he finds they're rushing a dying piglet to hospital.

Mr Betts (not seen in episode), the coalman, gives the Goods a retired horse to solve their transport problem.

4: I Talk to the Trees

Mr Wakeling (Noel Howlett), an old gardener that Tom and Barbara meet down at the allotments, talks to his plants and plays music to them, believing they grow better as a result. Although sceptical at first, Tom conducts some experiments to test out Mr Wakeling's theories.

Mr Chipchase (Raymond Mason) attends the extraordinary meeting of the local music society at Margo's house and sticks up for the absent Miss Mountshaft when Margo tries to usurp her position as president.

Madam Acting-Chairwoman (Joyce Windsor) chairs the music society meeting at the Leadbetters'.

5: The Windbreak War

Mr Bailey (Timothy Bateson) is the builder who installs Margo's new windbreak – in the wrong place.

Workman (Roger Pope): An unskilled labourer employed by Mr Bailey.

Workman (Desmond Cullum-Jones): Wally, who also works for Mr Bailey, helps erect the windbreak.

6: Whose Fleas are These?

Mr Bulstrode (Michael Robbins) is the council official who visits the Goods to investigate their flea problem. He's

been in the 'infestation' profession for years, and so has his son Mickey.

Postman (Ray Dunbobbin): The postman delivers a parcel to the Goods' house, only to be faced with some strange behaviour from Barbara, who's worried that she may give him fleas.

7: The Last Posh Frock

Eileen (Liz Robertson) is an old friend of Barbara's, now a model living in Canada. When she returns to England, Tom invites her to dinner, hoping to cheer up his downcast wife.

Man (Ronald Nunnery): Walking down The Avenue, he offends Barbara by calling her 'sonny'.

SERIES FOUR

1: Away from It All

Robert (not seen in episode) invites his friends the Leadbetters to make use of his smart Mayfair flat while he's in Tehran, but Jerry, in turn, loans the place to the Goods.

2: The Green Door

Mrs Holman (Jane Hilary), the owner of the local riding school, annoys Margo by giving Tom and Barbara permission to help themselves to horse manure.

Miss Harmsworth (Toria Fuller) runs the weight-watchers' class in the high street, which Margo has secretly been attending twice a week while pretending to go riding.

3: Our Speaker Today…

Lady Truscott (Angela Thorne), who's the guest of honour when Barbara gives her well-received talk on self-sufficiency to the local Townswomen's Guild, subsequently becomes friendly with the Goods and persuades Barbara to speak at further functions.

the poor woman has laryngitis so can't deliver her talk to the Townswomen's Guild.

Mrs Burke (not seen in episode) phones the Leadbetters' house and speaks to

IN THE BACKGROUND

Two of the most frequently talked-about people in the show were never seen. **MISS DOLLY MOUNTSHAFT** (who smelt of camphorated oil) and **MRS DOOMS-PATTERSON** were two of social-climber Margo's so-called friends – and yet she spent most of her time making snide comments about them behind their backs.

It's dangerous making rash judgements about people, but it doesn't take too much grey matter to realize that both characters – neither of whom Jerry could stand – were every bit as as snooty and shallow as Margo could be at times.

Dolly Mountshaft's claim to fame around the streets of Surbiton, where she owned a flatlet in the high street, was running the music society and choral singing classes, both of which Margo attended.

Meanwhile, like Margo, the corpulent Mrs Dooms-Patterson (weighing in at 20 stone) was a member of the local pony club, which was a source of much hilarity between Tom and Barbara. They even shared the joke with Mrs Holman, the owner of the stables, when they saw the size of the horse the woman rode. As well as being a riding pal of Margo's, Mrs Dooms-Patterson was the wife of the local Conservative agent and tried roping Margo in to help with local election campaigns.

Bus Conductor (Con Chambers): Conductor of the Kingston-bound bus that Tom chases when Lenin, his cockerel, escapes and jumps onto it.

Mr Batty (Colin McCormack) works at Grant Hall, a remand home, where Barbara gives her final talk.

Lad (Robert Lindsay): One of the lads at Grant Hall, who tells Tom why Barbara's talk was so popular with her young audience – she was wearing a transparent dress!

Mrs Wormwood (not seen in episode) is the librarian Margo accuses of stabbing her in the back, just because

Jerry, wanting to pass on her congratulations to Barbara for her talk.

4: The Weaver's Tale

Ernie (Milton Johns) works at the second-hand shop where Tom buys a loom.

5: Suit Yourself

Snetterton (Philip Madoc) is a colleague of Jerry's and his opponent in the battle for the managing director's chair.

Donald Dalby (Terence Conoley), also employed by JJM Ltd, is another contender for the MD's job, but hardly a favourite!

Mrs Dalby (Patricia Driscoll), Donald's wife, accompanies him to the get-together at the Fatted Calf, at which 'Sir' announces his retirement.

Mr Greaves (not seen in episode) owns the sheep farm where Tom and Barbara work in return for fleece.

CHRISTMAS SPECIAL (1977)

Silly, but it's Fun

Bill (David Battley) has to perform the unenviable task of delivering Margo's very precisely specified Christmas tree.

ROYAL COMMAND PERFORMANCE (1978)

When I'm 65

Mr Downs (George Cole) is the bank manager who turns Tom down when he proposes his 'infantile' retirement scheme.

Taxi Driver (Steve Ismay): Having driven Tom and Jerry home after drinking at the pub (when they should have been out running), he lets the cat out of the bag by returning with the wallet one of them inadvertently left behind.

IN FRONT OF THE QUEEN

It's not often that scriptwriters get the chance to write for royalty, but John Esmonde and Bob Larbey enjoyed this privilege back in 1978, on the occasion of a special performance of *The Good Life* recorded in the presence of Her Majesty The Queen. The event was in aid of the appeal to send teams from the British Isles to the Commonwealth Games at Edmonton, and Studio Six at Television Centre was packed with an invited audience joining the Queen and Prince Philip to watch the specially written episode, 'When I'm 65' – the first sitcom the royal visitors had ever seen recorded.

Being asked to write an episode specially for the Royal Command Performance (transmitted on Saturday, 10 June 1978) was a wonderful moment for the writers. 'I was deeply, deeply proud,' says John Esmonde. 'When we were told, Bob and I decided we wouldn't do any corgi jokes – I hate them. Her Majesty has to suffer them all the time and still smile. We'd simply write another *Good Life*. And it must have gone down well, because the Queen wrote to us afterwards, which thrilled me to bits.'

The writers' intention to keep this special episode in line with the rest of the plot was difficult to achieve, because the sitcom had already been brought to an end with the episode 'Anniversary', in which the Goods decided to soldier on in the face of adversity. As the Command Performance was to help the Commonwealth Games Appeal, the plot involved physical rivalry between Tom and Jerry. 'It worked quite well,' says Bob, 'and overall it was a very happy, albeit frightening, sort of evening.'

Bob, too, classed it an honour to have royalty watch the show. 'We were completing the last series when the producer first told us about it, and, of course, you don't say no to an offer like that, even though everyone was terrified when it came to the actual recording. I've never seen so many technicians around the BBC in the whole of my life. There seemed to be three electricians to every light bulb, just to make sure everything went smoothly.'

Life was hectic prior to the day of recording, and no one was busier than production manager Brian Jones, who was responsible, among other things, for liaising with other departments to ensure that the venue was shipshape. 'I also had to contact the owners of the houses in Kewferry Road to let them know what was happening. We didn't need to use the back gardens, everything was filmed out the front, and luckily the owners were happy about it,' says Brian.

Brian well remembers the day John Howard Davies announced the news. 'He pulled everyone together and told us the Queen was coming in June to see a special recording of the show. The reaction was total shock, with everyone saying, "You mean recording breaks?", and he said, "Yes." When someone shouted, "Retakes?", John again answered, "Yes." Then I heard, "Oh shit, so we're actually going to be making mistakes in front of the Queen," and John replied, "I'd be very disappointed, and surprised, if you didn't." '

With only a few weeks to go before the big event, Brian Jones was busy at Television Centre making sure everything was in tip-top condition for the royal visitors. 'John and I inspected the route the Queen would take, with one of the heads of department, and we agreed on all the areas that needed tidying up or painting, which included the flagpole. I remember John telling her, "We'll want commissionaires in their white gloves and uniforms." '

But Brian Jones' responsibilities didn't stop there – he was also badgered into being the warm-up artist for the night, charged with relaxing the audience prior to the evening's show. Although Brian had performed this task before, he didn't much relish doing it on the night the Queen was coming! 'John Howard Davies said, "You know the warm-up's due to be done by Richard Waring, because he's our senior warm-up man?" I acknowledged that fact and said I thought it was a good idea. "Well, he's not going to," John said. "Everybody feels that because you've done such a good job over the years, you should do it."

Everyone was shocked when it was announced that the Queen was coming to watch the show.

STANDING IN FOR THE QUEEN

During rehearsals an extra was hired to stand in for the Queen so that the cast and crew could practise their greetings and handshakes in preparation for the big occasion. But when she failed to turn up for the dress rehearsal, Penelope Keith's dresser, Celia McDowell, found herself landed with the job instead. 'They asked me because I'm the same height as the Queen,' says Celia, although she initially refused to do it, after one of her colleagues had jokingly remarked that she should wear a velvet gown and an artificial crown. 'I told them the Queen would turn up in a dress, which she did. There was no way I'd wear a gown and crown!'

One of Celia's responsibilities that day was to sit in the seat to be occupied by the Queen. 'It gave the cameramen the chance to position their shots correctly, but as soon as the scenes were finished I had to run down, change Penny, and return to my seat. It was hard work but great fun. Penny was my favourite artist, and she'd let me do everything for her. She's a wonderful person.'

"You want me to do it for the *Queen*?", I asked. John replied, "Not only that, it'll be transmitted." All I could manage to say was, "Oh, Christ!"

'He told me in front of all the crew and cast, and everybody was encouraging me by saying things like, "Oh, that's smashing, you'll be great." There was nothing to do but reluctantly agree,' smiles Brian, who admits to having been very nervous when the Queen first entered the studio. 'I thought, "Oh God, I'm on now." But I went on, did the warm-up, and luckily everything worked out well. Afterwards everyone – including the actors – told me how good it was. They were all very nice and I appreciated that.'

The emotions Brian was going through in the run-up to the Queen's arrival were picked up on by Kenneth Robinson, who wrote up the event for *The Observer*. His piece also acknowledged what a good job Brian had done: '...the floor manager gave a really polished warm-up that made us wonder what had happened to his stage fright.'

After the recording, when the Queen was introduced individually to the cast, the writers and members of the production team, John Esmonde was shaking with nerves. 'She certainly comes prepared and knows everything about you. She asked me what we could expect in the near future as far as other shows were concerned, and what came out was something like "Oh, ahh, ahh, ahh" rather than sparkling repartee. But her response was lovely – she quietly squeezed my hand to stop my nerves exploding, which was very reassuring.'

The episode was watched by 14 million people, achieving the level reached throughout most of the fourth series, but critical reaction was mixed. Alec Ramsden declared in the *Yorkshire Post* that the 'much-vaunted' episode had failed to live up to expectations. In his review he remarked that he thought a seven-minute conducted tour of the studio had been an unwarranted waste of time, but added: 'Thank goodness for the delectable Penelope Keith, who turned a below-par programme into something mildly humorous.' Overall, he felt that viewing figures would drop 'if this piece of inconsequential nonsense is to be the recipe for the future'.

Conversely, Kenneth Robinson wrote in *The Observer*: 'The show itself was so good that I kept forgetting to take my eyes off the monitor and watch either the actors on the set or the Queen's reactions.'

Although the episode cannot be regarded as one of the strongest Esmonde and Larbey wrote, it remains one of the most important in that it marked the final demise of much-loved characters Tom, Barbara, Margo and Jerry. Periodic repeats have since been warmly received, but no new tales from The Avenue were ever seen and even the second Christmas Special being suggested at the time failed to materialize.

LIVING
THE GOOD LIFE?

One reason why *The Good Life* won such a loyal band of supporters among Britain's fickle viewing public was that it dealt with such a familiar situation. When Tom Good first appeared on our screens rebelling against his lot in life, millions of viewers found themselves instantly empathizing with him. The perennial question 'Surely there's more to life than this?' is a universal one, posed all the time by people fed up with competing in the rat race of commerce. The day-to-day stresses of battling against hordes of commuters and the relentless treadmill of a menial or dead-end job can take their toll, and many dream of finding an escape route by which to climb, once and for all, out of the employment rut.

Such issues are the nub of Esmonde and Larbey's sitcom, adroitly explored through the lives of the Goods. For Tom Good, reaching forty is the point at which he starts focusing on what he really wants out

of life. Sacrificing his precious time crawling along in the City rush-hour every morning, only to spend all day at a desk designing plastic animals for cereal packets in return for a paltry salary, has long since lost its appeal.

After chewing the matter over with his devoted wife Barbara, Tom decides that the only answer is a whole new way of life in the form of self-sufficiency

– never having to worry about anything but one another and the caprices of Nature. By the time the episode 'Anniversary' was transmitted, the Goods were celebrating two years of self-sufficiency. Such a radical change of lifestyle might not appeal to everyone, but it struck a loud chord with those yearning to turn their own lives around.

In fact, the influence of *The Good Life* was such that it induced many people to try their own hand at self-sufficiency – as Richard Briers' fan mail proved at the time. But most disciples of the Goods' exploits in The Avenue simply dabbled, continuing to derive their main income from just the sort of lifestyle that Tom had turned his back on, while others had ventured into self-sufficiency long before Tom and Barbara were ever conceived.

Being self-sufficient in suburbia is probably all but impossible in real life, but a rural setting offers the scope to cultivate enough land to produce adequate

• Many people regard 84-year-old **JOHN SEYMOUR** as the doyen of self-sufficiency. The author of several books on the subject (notably *The Complete Book of Self-Sufficiency*, which has been translated into fifteen languages and sold over half a million copies), he turned to self-sufficiency way back in 1948. 'During the war I served in the King's African Rifles, and when I returned I worked as a labour officer for the East Suffolk War Agricultural Committee for three years, finding farm work for German and Italian PoWs. When they finally went home I gave up the job, and I haven't worked for anyone since.'

John Seymour's leanings towards a life of self-sufficiency stem from living in Central Africa for thirteen years. 'If you lived in Central Africa in those days, you had to be self-sufficient. There wasn't a shop within 500 miles, and no roads or cars, so you walked everywhere. I got into the habit of being self-reliant, and when I came back to England after the

Millions of TV viewers felt an empathy with Tom and Barbara's desire to find a better way of life.

quantities of home-grown produce. Even so, most people who try fending for themselves are forced to fall back on working for a cottage industry or taking a part-time job in order to manage. Summoning up sufficient frugality and enterprise, not to mention carrying out enough hard manual labour, to survive entirely on home-produced supplies is no easy feat. Nevertheless, there are people who have given it their best shot and succeeded – to varying degrees.

war ended, I couldn't return to a life of popping along to the shop every time I needed an egg. I found it degrading and wouldn't do it, so I started producing my own food.'

Anyone embarking on a life of self-reliance today faces an uphill struggle, John believes. 'I still get lots of letters from people who've read one of my books and say they've always dreamed of being self-sufficient, but, sadly, for most of them it will only ever be a dream.

'The price of land is astronomical now. About five years ago in Ireland it used to be quite cheap, but not any more. It's very difficult setting yourself up with enough land to live off.' In recent years, John has noticed a trend towards buying smallholdings in France. 'A lot of people have tried their luck over there,' he says, 'partly because the planning laws aren't as draconian as they are in Britain.'

Before moving to Ireland, John lived a life of total self-sufficiency on a farm in Pembrokeshire. These days, however, a lack of land means there are some essentials he has to buy locally, much to his chagrin. 'We haven't enough land to grow our own wheat, so we have to buy flour. But we make our own butter and cheese, milk a cow, grow vegetables and produce all our own pork and beef. However, things are very much on a reduced scale nowadays – after all, I'm getting on a bit!'

Home for John Seymour is a remote farmhouse, situated on the banks of a river, miles from the nearest road, which he shares with his partners, Angela Ashe and Will Sutherland. 'We make our own small community, which includes the animals as well as Will and Angela's three children. Angela and I found the place over twenty years ago. She's an Irish girl who wanted to return to Ireland. We made a very effective working team and became good friends, then we met up with Will about seven years ago, and when he and Angela got together and decided to have a family, they wanted to continue with a self-sufficient lifestyle,' explains John.

'I don't need much money because we still produce most of our own food and provide our own water and firewood. But I've done a little work in the past for the BBC, and I interview people from time to time for RTE in Ireland. I also write books, which

brings me in a bit of income. And in the summer we run courses on self-sufficiency. People stay with neighbours who operate bed and breakfast, and come along every morning to learn about everything from milking a cow to making cider, cheese and butter.'

John is separated from his wife, Sally, who now lives on an 18-acre estate in Australia's New South Wales, but they still keep in touch. 'Sally had very similar ideas to mine, and still produces most of her own food.'

John has never been tempted to alter his self-sufficient lifestyle, even though he admits old age is beginning to take its toll. 'Within the last year my eyesight has deteriorated, which is very frustrating, and I'm also getting a little bit lazy. I don't want to milk a cow twice a day any more, and all the weeding and digging can be pretty hard going. Luckily, my two partners are keen to keep up the work, although we gave milking a miss this year as Angela has enough to do with two little babies to look after.

'Our heifer is in calf right now and I expect we'll be milking again in time for our courses next year. It's encouraging to find so many people from all walks of life who want to know how to grow their own food. There's no denying it can be hard work, but if you make a real go of it, there's nothing better than living off the land.'

• What must it be like to grow up in an environment of self-sufficiency, devoid of all the commercial trappings of modern-day living? JANE SEYMOUR, John Seymour's daughter, sometimes felt isolated. 'Because of the lifestyle we led, I felt different from the other children at school. I didn't feel as if I fitted in with them. Children have a need to belong to a social group, and if you stand out, other kids are quick to pick on you.' Jane remembers many such occasions during her schooldays. 'The other children used to tease me over the way I dressed, and the fact that my mother wore pigtails and sandals while all their mums had perms and high heels.

'My parents were probably looked on as cranks, and even my schoolfriends thought they were weird and eccentric. But when you're young, you don't really think too much about what your parents are doing and how their lifestyle is different from other people's. However, my friends loved "hanging out" at our farm, riding the horses and helping with the animals. There was always something exciting going on and loads of unusual people came to stay with us.'

Looking back, Jane feels she had an interesting childhood. 'Yes, there were downsides, but I don't think there's anything I would change, and I now feel privileged to have been brought up the way I was. There were times when, for example, people at school would be talking about their favourite television programme, and I felt I had very little to offer because we didn't own a TV set. But we didn't need television for entertainment – we had horses, and they were my life. I was more or less left to my own devices, so I'd ramble through the woods exploring the local countryside, which was lovely. We spent our evenings reading, talking or making things. Both my parents encouraged me to be creative.'

The ability to survive off the land depended on everyone pitching in, and Jane had regular chores to do. 'I'd help pick the potatoes, milk the cows and things like that, although I'm sure I complained a lot! We always had good food, though. It might not have been tins of baked beans, but we ate very well and healthily.'

Jane (who lives on a small farm in East Clare in the Republic of Ireland, in a house she and her husband built themselves) has only now started following in her parents' footsteps, but she's determined not to make the mistakes she feels they made. 'I felt they took on too much. I don't want to work so hard that I begin neglecting the relationship I have with my husband, Mike.

'If you have a nine-to-five job you can leave your work behind, but when you're living a self-sufficient life you never get away from it. We love living here in Ireland where it's peaceful and quiet, and I feel that producing as much food as you can organically is extremely important, especially these days, but you also have to keep matters in perspective and appreciate that there are other things in life equally as important as growing your own food – relationships with others, for example. It's not worth getting too serious about things.'

Nowadays, Jane makes a living teaching at evening classes and running her own pottery, but these are not skills nurtured at school, partly because she regularly played truant. 'I spent most of my school years mitching, so I never qualified in anything and never went to college. I loathed school and resented any time spent there.

'My father was always running down schools, saying how children get forced into these human sausage machines and come out exactly like everyone else. When he found out that I was mitching, I don't think he really minded too much. So it's taken quite a few years of trying this and that to discover that I enjoy making pots. Although my mother, Sally, is a potter, which has obviously influenced me, I'm very much self-taught. I can't say this is how I'll live the rest of my life, but at the moment it feels like the right thing to do.'

• A 15p postcard changed the whole life of **JOHN BARNES**. 'I'd already decided my job wasn't for me when I saw a postcard in the newsagent's window. It showed a man sitting at his desk looking out of a window, thinking: "Some day soon, I'm going to start living." John bought the postcard, and from that moment knew he had to alter his life.

Although *The Good Life* wasn't the driving force behind John and Dorothy Barnes' decision to quit their jobs and live a spartan existence in Wales, it did play its part. 'We'd seen the programme and thought it was excellent. It was on our wavelength and enthused us,' says John, who used to work as a parts manager while his wife was PA to a company director. 'We both gave up good jobs and a lot of money, but when you get hooked on something, that doesn't seem to matter any more.'

When the Barneses moved from Bromley into a run-down three-bedroomed property nine miles from Lampeter in West Wales in 1979, their friends thought they were mad, as John recalls. 'People thought we were absolutely bonkers giving up jobs and a house and moving two hundred miles to live on our own with no money coming in. But I knew it was something we had to do, or we'd regret it. Dorothy was twenty-nine, I was thirty and we didn't have kids, so it was the perfect time to try it.'

Deciding to alter the course of their lives was more than just a whim, it was an idea that took three years to incubate. 'It took that long to actually achieve our move, from the time we started seriously thinking about it to finding a suitable place in Wales. Six months before leaving my job I had a word with my boss and gave him six months' notice – which was more than was necessary. In return, I asked for every Friday off so that I could drive to Wales on Thursday night, freeing up the whole weekend for our house-hunting.'

Knowing it was imperative that they kept their expenditure to a minimum, the Barneses knew they had to buy a property outright. The sale of their house in Bromley made this possible, and they found their new home quite quickly. 'We were lucky,' John admits. 'At that time there were lots of people with the same idea, so we had to move fast. The place we bought had only just come onto the market.'

Dorothy had circularized all the estate agents in South and West Wales with their requirements, and details of a suitable property arrived back at Bromley while John was busy searching in Wales. A well-timed phone call from Dorothy to a house John was in the process of viewing resulted in their finding their dream home. 'The old lady who owned it had only used one room,' says John. 'The rest of the house hadn't been lived in for about six years and was in a state. So was the only toilet – out in the back garden, it was simply a plank of wood with a hole cut into it and a bucket underneath!'

John spent six months making the house habitable before Dorothy – who had been temping to earn the money to buy a Rayburn, which she says turned out to be 'the centre of their future' – joined him. Within two days of moving in, his wife was thrown in at the deep end. 'A neighbour asked her to help save a ewe that was experiencing difficulties lambing. We'd done a course in lambing beforehand, but doing it for real was a different matter, especially when a few days earlier you'd been working in the City!'

After a great deal of toil and sweat, the Barneses began to reap the benefits. 'We had a vegetable patch, goats, chicken, sheep, and all the local farmers got to know me, offering work whenever they needed an extra pair of hands.' But while John was living his life-long dream, Dorothy was finding her eighteen-hour days spent in isolation a nightmare.

Living in such a remote area nearly had tragic consequences for the couple when their baby daughter developed meningitis. The reality of being in the middle of nowhere, thirty miles from the nearest hospital, suddenly hit home. 'Victoria was only nine weeks old when she contracted the illness, and she was on the critical list for seven days. The doctors told my wife she'd got her there just in time,' John remembers.

Averting this near-tragedy had a lasting effect on the Barneses, and in 1983 they packed their bags and headed for Bournemouth. After staying with friends for a while, the couple now have their own home, and for John life has turned full circle because he's employed, once again, as a parts manager in a garage. But self-sufficiency is still a passion. 'I run evening classes on the subject at Bournemouth and Poole, and don't rule out trying again,' says John, who is now fifty. 'Perhaps in five years' time I'll retire to the country and have another go.'

Whenever *The Good Life* is repeated, John enjoys watching, partly because it brings back memories of the life he left behind. Despite its being only a sit-com, he regards it as 'pretty accurate', although, as he observes, 'Some things wouldn't have worked, like having only one goat. It's virtually impossible keeping just one because they need contact with others. And having one pig is, I think, a little unfair because it needs some form of companionship. But other than that, everything they did was perfectly feasible.'

• For **HEATHER THOMAS** (31) and **MARK LOMAS** (36), living on a redundant piece of bog-land twenty miles from Limerick was the ideal way of escaping the pressures of modern-day life. 'Trying to keep a £60,000 mortgage going, running two cars and a truck, and simply existing became too much,' explains Heather. 'We were working seven days a week for the mortgage company, had negative equity on the house and didn't have any sort of life. We became quite depressed and had to do something about it.'

Heather had grown up on her parents' farm in Cornwall and harboured dreams of returning to that way of life. Her partner, a self-employed builder, came to share the same desire, having himself been

brought up on allotment culture in Yorkshire. But they knew that land in England – especially Kent, where they lived – was too expensive and the planning controls too restrictive, so they looked overseas. 'We spent five years planning a move to France. We really did our homework, deciding how much land we could afford and where the best place was, only to discover that it was full of English people already, playing cricket and things like that – everything we wanted to get away from.'

Then a friend suggested the West of Ireland, where the beauty of the countryside was still intact and the cost of land still low. After spotting an estate agent's advertisement for property in County Clare in a magazine, Heather and Mark bought a ferry ticket and travelled to Eire. They stayed for just three days,

but that gave them enough time to put in an offer on a piece of land. Five months later they had packed their two dogs and two cats (and some illicit apple trees and garden tools) into an old caravan and were heading for a new life.

That was five years ago, but Heather and Mark are still living in a 14-foot touring caravan with timber additions. 'It's taken all this time to save enough money to build our own house,' says Mark, who is currently building them an eco-friendly, solar-powered, three-bedroomed house with timber frames, recycled insulation and 'breathing' walls and roof. After enduring such a long time in a caravan designed for no more than two-week holidays, people are amazed that the couple are not tearing their hair out. 'There haven't been too many arguments,' smiles

Far left: Heather Thomas with her horse, Coco.

Left: Heather and her first batch of kids.

Below: For over five years, home was a 14-foot caravan.

Mark. 'We spent five years in a two-up, two-down in Kent, so we're used to living in a small space – and we're both committed to this.'

Their little patch of Ireland was far from top quality because it had been stripped of peat, which had been used for burning, but it was all they could afford. For the first two years they claimed Social Security benefit while trying to realize their dreams and become totally self-sufficient. 'We wanted to live off the land, and in the second year felt we had everything we needed, including our own transport in the shape of a horse and cart as well as bicycles, and we were eating our own totally organic food – meat, milk, cheese, yogurt, fruit and eggs. We were also generating all our own electricity from wind and solar power, and cutting our own fuel for heating.

Only about £10 a week was being spent on essentials like animal feed and toilet rolls. And we've never been fitter or healthier.'

Although they've survived five years in what many would regard as bleak surroundings, Heather and Mark admit that it's been a long learning curve. 'We came over intending to live as cheaply as possible because we had very little money,' says Heather. 'We didn't go out and buy expensive milking goats, we bought the best we could afford. And we wanted to try and live without the pressure of household bills.

'But there are some things we shouldn't have tried doing all at once. We bought chickens, goats and a pig without having anything to feed them with, and ended up spending almost as much on feeding the animals as feeding ourselves.'

The harsh realities of living on bogland forced Heather and Mark to revise their plans regarding living entirely off the land. 'That hasn't worked because our land isn't really suitable,' admits Heather. 'We sold our horses because we don't have enough land to keep them and cut hay. We've decided to move away from the idea of total self-sufficiency and selling produce for cash, cut off from everyone else. Now we run a 'green' business, sharing the knowledge we've built up by advising people on subjects like eco-friendly housing and designing reed beds for wastewater treatment. And we also hope to set up a wetland plant nursery, which means using the land to grow what it's best suited for – permaculture has taught us that.'

Life has been far from idyllic, with the inclement weather taking its toll. 'We never realized how

Heather Thomas with her pig, Cynthia, who suffered from sunburnt ears.

important a part the weather played in our lives,' says Mark, 'until we came over here and had to spend so much time out in it. There are always things to do but sometimes you can't get out there because the land is too wet. It can be quite frustrating.'

But neither of them regrets their decision. 'No way!' Mark exclaims. 'We don't have a mortgage, that's the difference. Everything we've got, we've earned. One day the thought struck me that here we are, owning a few acres of our own land and our own detached home outright. We keep horses, have a sailing boat, eat the best organic food, breathe the freshest air, drink the finest Irish spring water, and don't have a pot to pee in – literally!

'As it happens, the Irish economy has boomed and the value of our property has increased dramatically. We still produce most of our own food and live well, albeit on a limited budget, thanks to the income from a worthwhile and satisfying small business.'

Heather is equally proud of their achievements. 'The freedom to do whatever you want is wonderful,' she enthuses. 'Life is more difficult in many ways, such as working longer hours, but we're doing it for ourselves, and that's the difference.'

Whereas lots of people fall by the wayside pursuing their dream of a more self-sufficient lifestyle, Heather Thomas and Mark Lomas have succeeded by compromising whenever necessary and not being overdogmatic. 'A lot of people are very enthusiastic and want to do everything, but within a few months they're fed up with the way of life. When we first moved here our letters home were full of things like how we'd helped a farmer pull a cow out of a ditch and he'd revived it with poteen, not going to the pub until nearly closing time for music sessions, and donning wellies just to go to the toilet. Those sort of things have become commonplace now, but I still wake up in the morning and think, "Wow! This is great!" When it's frosty, there's a mist over the bogland, or you spot heron, kingfishers or otters, you realize it's an amazing place to live. This really is "the good life".'

Heather and Mark have encountered mixed reactions from their friends and relatives. 'Our families have been very supportive, they're just pleased that we're doing something that makes us happy. It's old college friends who think we're potty. Two friends visited last year but they refuse to come back until we've got electric lighting and a flushing toilet! Inevitably, one of them became known as Margo from the time we grew our first cabbage in Kent, and she relishes the nickname.'

When considering the merits of *The Good Life* as an accurate document on self-sufficiency, Heather and Mark are sceptical. 'As a comedy show it was great,' says Heather, 'but there's no way you could live with just a garden. You need at least five to ten acres to realistically keep livestock and grow all their fodder. But we enjoyed the show, and if all it did was persuade some people to plant a row of lettuce in their back garden or rent an allotment, it's done some good.'

'Tom and Barbara's relationship was realistic,' comments Mark. 'You need a strong relationship to survive, and you have to be good friends.'

• When **LYN THOMAS** took her first bath in ten months, she declared it better than sex! 'We spent seven weeks looking for our dream home in France, and when we finally found it there was lots of work needed.' The property was in such a state of disrepair that Lyn and her husband, Edward, spent six months sharing a portaloo in a barn with a stray cat and her kitten. So when – on 31 October 1997 – Lyn finally got to relax among the soap suds, it felt like heaven.

For Lyn, living off the land had been a lifetime's ambition and she can't remember whether Tom and Barbara Good's adventures were an influence. 'I

For Lyn Thomas, living off the land is a dream come true.

always dreamt of "living off the land", but then I had four small children and a husband who thought I was crackers.' Now, years later, she's enjoying life in France and has succeeded in becoming as self-reliant as possible.

'With all my children married and settled, and a new husband – who's just as crackers as me – in 1997

Edward Thomas surveys the house in France that took seven weeks to find!

we sold up and set off for France, where land is plentiful and cheap. We bought a dilapidated farm cottage with barns and set about renovating it. Now, when we sit in front of our log-burning fire at night reading, listening to Radio 4 or indulging in one of our many hobbies, we consider ourselves very lucky. We're certainly living "the good life".'

It's now two years since Lyn and Edward Thomas left North Wales and crossed the channel to Brittany, and they wouldn't give up their new-found lifestyle for anything. 'It's hasn't been easy and money is tight, but we'd never go back to the rat race. Every room in our cottage is only part-finished, but when they're ready we plan offering bed and breakfast to earn some money.'

Their two acres of land have now been ploughed for the first time in twenty years, and fruit trees, bushes and vegetables are being planted as part of their drive for self-sufficiency. Even though buying a place in the country and being independent had always been a dream, it was a combination of circumstances that drove Lyn and Edward to give it a go. 'My husband, who's an accountant, was made redundant. We wanted to buy some land but couldn't afford to in Wales. While holidaying over here we saw lots of affordable properties with land,' says Lyn, who used to run her own accountancy firm as well as a chutney-making business.

Having decided to take the plunge, as soon as they returned from holiday they placed their house on the market – and within five weeks it was sold. Before moving, Lyn phoned her children, from whom she received nothing but encouragement. 'They all said: "You've only got one life and we're all married and settled, so go for it!" There were only two people who thought us mad.'

In France, Lyn, now 55, and Edward, 57, knew exactly what sort of property they wanted, but looked at almost fifty before finding it. 'We wanted somewhere out of town, but not too far, a place that wasn't too isolated and somewhere that had a decent roof, because that's costly to repair. We were also looking for a place that had a couple of acres of land, with water and electricity in the house. We finally found one, costing 120,000 francs.'

Not all Brits who try life in France can stand the pace. Many see things through rose-tinted spectacles instead of fitting in with the realities – a scenario that Lyn (who is planning to write her own cookbook based on chestnut recipes) and Edward have seen all too often. 'People spend a couple of weeks here in midsummer and think it's wonderful. But our advice to anyone considering such a move is to rent somewhere between October and the end of March so as to experience living here during the winter. Then, if you still like it after that, take it from there.'

Although they grow as much food as possible, as well as keeping their own chickens, ducks, goats and sheep, the couple admit that they're not entirely self-sufficient. 'There are certain things you can't grow. Edward likes coffee, for example, so we have to buy

The Thomases' dream home
has taken a lot of hard work
and money to get shipshape.
Below: Henrietta the hen
catches a mouse.

that. And everything takes so much time. It takes ages to build up an orchard so that you can grow fruit and establish your own nut trees, but we'll get there.'

Money remains tight, but Lyn and Edward intend to stay on in France. 'Other than our family, of course, there's nothing we miss about Britain. And the thought of joining the nine-to-five routine again, and working in an office, drives us mad.'

Once they've finished renovating their home,
Lyn and Edward plan offering bed and breakfast.

WRITING
SITCOMS

Just like the British climate, the world of sitcom-writing is unpredictable. Moods and styles are perpetually changing, which makes the market-place difficult to read. Decision-makers at the television companies struggle to find the perfect riposte to the question they're increasingly asked: 'Why don't they make them like that any more?' On the whole, today's situation comedy scripts tend to be made up of hard-hitting, blatant dialogue, often full of expletives and lavatorial humour. Desperate for a laugh a line, writers have taken the risk of producing shallow, faceless characters – with the result that the genre has taken a battering from the critics in recent times.

Sadly, it seems there's no longer room in the TV schedules for shows based on gentle humour, allowing viewers time to understand and grow fond of characters, or letting the laughter come from the situation rather than the dialogue alone. Scriptwriters seem to be focusing increasingly on younger audiences, leaving fans of more mature sitcoms with very little to satisfy their appetite. But if this is really what the public demands nowadays, why is it that so many classics – from *Dad's Army* and *Hi-De-Hi!* to *Steptoe and Son* and *The Good Life* – continue pulling in such large audiences?

Some writers seem to feel that just about every situation has already been covered in sitcom, so their only viable alternative is to resort to scenarios that are just too fantastic or wild to reflect real life. But Bob Larbey doesn't see it that way. 'Every new generation of writers thinks everything has been covered already, but it never has. As time passes, there are always new things to say. My only grumble with a lot of current material is that it's "in your face" comedy, where the writers try far too hard to be upfront and funny.

'You get some people who try to be outrageous all the time. It's almost as if they're thinking, "What's the next shocking thing we can do?" That bothers me a bit – but perhaps I'm just an old fogey, or simply

stuck in a gentler age of comedy. But something as good as *Dad's Army* was never forced on you, it never pushed you into your chair and said, "We'll shock you into laughter, if necessary." It just sort of crept over you like a nice warm blanket.'

People have frequently used the term 'gentle' to describe Esmonde and Larbey's style of comedy, but it's a tag disliked by John Esmonde. 'I would never use the word about anything, I hate it But there you go! I think our writing was more about the psychology of the characters. It's psychological writing in the sense of the comedy coming from mental quirks – recognizable, I hope, by the British public.'

Television today differs considerably from the days when Esmonde and Larbey were submitting ideas, a point which John reluctantly acknowledges. 'Whenever we had an idea for a show, it was simply a case of providing a verbal synopsis of the idea. Then, if the

decision-makers at the TV station liked it, they'd say, "Go away and write it." It was as simple as that.'

Esmonde and Larbey stuck with the genre of sitcoms throughout their writing careers because it suited them from a financial and personal viewpoint. 'In the beginning, we were steered towards it by people wiser than us, who believed we were capable of writing more than just sketches. I'm not knocking anybody who *does* only do that, but people thought we should write longer and broader,' explains Bob.

'Once we got into writing situation comedies, it suited us perfectly. The trouble is, we began thinking life was made up of half-hour episodes!' he smiles. 'But the money's good for sitcoms, whereas to make a living out of sketches or gags you have to work like stink. With sitcoms there's such a range of subjects to cover. You'll never be short of ideas – though whether you manage to sell them is another matter.'

When it comes to identifying the essential ingredients of good situation comedy, quality characters are at the top of Bob Larbey's list. 'We learnt as we went along that if you could get the audience liking your characters – or indeed disliking them, but at least getting involved in some way – that was a key element. People have got to think of your characters as almost real, as though they're visiting their home for half an hour every week.' And, as Bob points out, 'If you get that right, you've got a bedrock on which the programme can grow.'

John, meanwhile, feels that success hinges on the quality of the writing. 'You need a good script. A bad one can't be saved even by a great performance. You can have a tremendous actor playing the lead, trying to compensate for grotty work, but gradually it'll throttle him or her. Once you have a decent script, you need a collective willingness between the actors,

writers and director to make it the best thing you've ever done. You have to care about it, because cynicism shows up.'

For some time there has been a debate about the influx of American shows. Still being imported, these are regarded by some as superior to home-grown offerings. Bob Larbey is a fan of some such shows. 'Frasier is wonderfully written. There have always been some good American comedies around. Even in the days when everyone said Americans couldn't write sitcoms, we had M*A*S*H, Cheers and Barney Miller. Obviously there's an awful lot of rubbish as well, but something like Frasier is as good as anything we've got over here at the moment, because it's character-driven. It's also clean, witty and dares to do jokes that not everybody will understand. I love that. For most of my professional life I've thought there was always something good coming out of America.'

INDEX